DO YOU REMEMBER ...?

Recollections and Reflections
on the last 21 Years of
the Egypt General Mission
in Egypt – 1935-56

One retired missionary (Aubrey Whitehouse)
writes to a retired contemporary (Alan Tucker)

Arthur Jeffery Centre for the Study of Islam
Melbourne School of Theology
An affiliated college of the Australian College of Theology

Do you remember ...?: Recollections and Reflections on the last 21 Years of the Egypt General Mission in Egypt – 1935-56
Aubrey Whitehouse

ISBN - 978-0-9876154-3-5

© 2017 Melbourne School of Theology Press. All rights reserved.

Editor
Ruth Nicholls

Production and Cover Design
Ho-yuin Chan

Publishing Services
Published by MST Press
Thanks to Richard Shumack for his publishing services.

Arthur Jeffery Centre for the Study of Islam
Melbourne School of Theology
5 Burwood Highway, Wantirna, Victoria, 3152, Australia.
PO Box 6257, Vermont South, Victoria, 3133, Australia
Ph: +61 3 9881 7800, Fax: +61 3 9800 0121
info@JefferyCentre.mst.edu.au
www.mst.edu.au

Opinions and conclusions published are those of the author and do not necessarily represent the views of the Arthur Jeffery Centre for the Study of Islam or its Editors. The Melbourne School of Theology Press affirms the free expression of the religious convictions of its authors but rejects hatred towards any persons or religious group.

Contents

The Editor's Foreword	5
Introducing Aubrey H Whitehouse	11
Acknowledgements	15
By Way of Explanation	19
Junior Missionaries –	21
Fellow-Workers	31
Believers from Muslim backgrounds	45
The War Years – 1939-1945	57
Institutions	63
Missions and Government	81
Good-bye, Egypt	89
Retrospect	97

The Editor's Foreword

Serendipitous is a word that a friend of mine often uses for those divinely initiated events which come together in a unique way resulting in the unexpected. In this case, it was a simple email to the Director of the Arthur Jeffery Centre for the Study of Islam, Melbourne School of Theology that simply asked, "Would you be interested in the reflections of Aubrey Whitehouse?". The answer was, "Let's have a look at it." Who is Aubrey Whitehouse and why would the Arthur Jeffery Centre for the Study of Islam be interested in possibly publishing his reflections?

Aubrey graduated from the Melbourne Bible Institute in 1935. Almost immediately, it would seem, Aubrey left for Egypt, where he was to serve with the Egypt General Mission until 1956, when British missionaries were expelled from the country. Later, he became the Principal of the Lebanon Bible Institute. (It was about that time that the Egypt General Mission became the Middle East General Mission.)[1] Aubrey become fluent in Arabic and since much of his work was with Muslims he became a student of Islam. While in Egypt he was busy preparing materials that were suitable for use in ministry to Muslims.

Aubrey, with his wife Elsie, retired to Melbourne, where one of the many avenues of service that were opened to him was lecturing in Islam at the Bible College of Victoria (previously Melbourne Bible Institute; now Melbourne School of Theology). The Principal at the time, Rev Neville Anderson, who himself had served for many years in Bangladesh, (also a country with a considerable Muslim population) would have understood the need for Christians to be equipped for effective ministry to Muslims. So then, Aubrey Whitehouse was one of a number of people who have lectured in subjects related to Islam at the college. Such foundations as these ultimately resulted in the formation in 2007

---

[1] The Middle East General Mission together with the Lebanon Evangelical Mission became Middle East Christian Outreach in 1976.

of the Centre for the Study of Islam and Other Faiths under the Directorship of Professor Peter Riddell, himself a scholar of Islam. With the increasing interest and focus on Islam, the Centre was renamed the Arthur Jeffery Centre for the Study of Islam in 2016.

In addition, the resultant research arising from that email has unearthed a valuable legacy of materials by Whitehouse relating to Islam. In the MST library, there is a detailed and annotated Bibliography on works relating to Islam. While dated (it was completed in 1984), it is an invaluable resource for a person who is interested in older studies of Islam. One of Whitehouse's most significant academic contributions is his select translation of an Arabic work which is entitled in English *A Topical Concordance to the Qur'an*. Another is a small booklet entitled *What the Qur'an Says* which was printed by the Fellowship of Faith for Muslims, UK.

Having been involved in theological education by extension, it is not surprising that Whitehouse wrote several courses: his *Introduction to Islam* uses that format. Using his experience in Egypt he also prepared a *Basic Arabic* course which was accompanied by cassettes. As for these significant materials that have come to light – and here I acknowledge the help of John Wood, the sender of the initial email – the Arthur Jeffery Centre for the Study of Islam, Melbourne School of Theology has decided that Whitehouse's writings are too valuable to be lost. So, the plan is to publish not only his *Reflections* but also several of his other works.

While his reflections are dated, an additional significance for the Arthur Jeffery Centre is that Whitehouse was one of Arthur Jeffery's Arabic students. Secondly, Whitehouse reflects on various aspects of Christian interaction with Muslims and finally he also comments on and at times questions the methods that were accepted in his time. His work then provides thoughtful reflection on Christian engagement with Muslims from which every generation could benefit.

Finally, this collection is a personal story so it is essentially biographical. It is also historical and so like the Acts of the Apostles it tells the story of God's work in one small area of Egypt. Like the Acts of the Apostles it points to the workings of the Holy Spirit. So, my recommendation is, read this book. It's worth it.

Ruth Nicholls
Administrator
Arthur Jeffery Centre for the Study of Islam

Aubrey and Elsie Whitehouse on the occasion of their 50th Wedding Anniversary, 10th June, 1990, Melbourne

Introducing Aubrey H Whitehouse

Aubrey Whitehouse was born in NSW, Australia on the 18th April 1908. As a young man, he trained as a structural draftsman. He arrived in Egypt in 1935, aged 27, as an accepted missionary recruit of the then Egypt General Mission (EGM). His South Australian missionary colleague Lester Williams strongly encouraged him to write his "Recollections and Reflections", something which Aubrey resisted for some time. Finally, he decided to draft them as a letter, calling for comment, to his contemporary in Egypt, Alan Tucker, a New Zealander. Another contemporary was Noel Hunt, also from New Zealand, who also became a close friend and features in the account from time to time. In a short reply, Alan Tucker recalls so much of what was written and vouches for its truthfulness.

Stationed at EGM Headquarters, Ezbet el-Zeitoun, a part of Cairo's northeast outskirts, Aubrey was enrolled for the full-time study of Arabic and Muslim culture at the School of Oriental Studies of Cairo University, also known as the American University, since it was founded by the American Presbyterian Mission.

Aubrey's missionary career had three distinct phases – four, if you wish to include his continuing activity after retirement from overseas. These were Egypt 1935-1956, Eritrea 1957-1959, Lebanon 1960-1971 and Melbourne, Australia, 1971 until his death on 26 March 1997.

Egypt
Aubrey became immersed in a deep study of the Arabic language and Egyptian/Muslim culture, which he relished and which would characterise all his future work. In due course, he was posted to the moderately large EGM hospital as an evangelist/administrator, situated further north east into the Delta, at Shebin-el-Kanater. He was there for at least ten years and remained connected until EGM was expelled from Egypt in 1956

as were all British personnel as part of the Suez Canal Crisis. His main responsibilities were to plan the program, for preaching and teaching, in the wards and outpatient area, in which all medical staff participated, distributing Arabic Christian literature including Scriptures as well as scheduling visits to the village of any patient who had appeared significantly interested while at the hospital. This interest was finally assessed by a discharge interview, planned and carried out by Aubrey and others. He was also called upon to talk with patients or relatives who had problems. Providing for staff prayer meetings also fell to his lot. Administratively, he was also responsible for managing the finances, including banking and the payment of wages. In these recollections, you will read of many who found Christ and also of the excellent teamwork of the Egyptian Christians whom Aubrey admired. Not surprisingly, prayer was a significant aspect of the work and Aubrey shared that commitment.

Aubrey had deep concerns for those from Islam, who in finding Christ had been rejected by their family and expelled by their village. How could they support themselves? Would they find a Christian woman willing to marry them? These concerns led, after the War, to the Farm Colony Bible College.

World War II saw Aubrey and his wife, Elsie, whom he had married on the field in 1940, extend free hospitality to many, many British servicemen in Egypt. Together with their colleagues they contributed to their moral and spiritual welfare, while keeping up their mission commitments.

Eritrea
In January 1957 those EGMer's expelled from Egypt met in London for prayer and to consider reports about possible new fields. Aubrey and Alan Tucker were commissioned to visit Eritrea and confer with other missions there. As a result, Eritrea was chosen as the new field with the EGM now taking the name of Middle East General Mission and the first five missionaries arrived in Asmara in October 1957 where a building was rented as HQ. Aubrey became the first Field Leader and helped to pioneer clinics and schools in the far west at Tessenei and Makboola. In this connection, he did a number of rugged outdoor "safaris" by Landrover with his colleagues. However, after two years, he and Elsie were seconded to Lebanon Evangelical Mission for work in the Lebanon Bible Institute.

Lebanon

Aubrey joined the staff of LBI in 1961 as a lecturer. The LBI had been reopened by Les de Smidt in 1952, and in 1963 it moved from old premises in Shemlan to new premises in Beirut. When de Smidt left in 1964, (to become Field Leader in 1965), Aubrey became Principal. Under his leadership, a TEE (Theological Education by Extension) program was added. As a member of a joint committee, LBI was assisting with the translation of the IVF Bible Commentary into Arabic. In addition, a weekly Christian Arabic radio program began to be aired over a number of Christian short wave radio stations broadcasting into the Middle East and surrounding countries. This brought favourable response from many listeners but for Aubrey it was a very time-consuming and demanding Project. In 1971 Aubrey felt it was time to retire and he and Elsie took up residence in Melbourne, Australia.

Retirement

Aubrey and Elsie attended the Church of All Nations where services and sermons where provided simultaneously with translation into a number of languages, Arabic being one. They ministered to the associated Arabic speaking group of believers, midweek and Sundays. Aubrey was also invited by the then Principal of Melbourne Bible Institute, Neville Andersen, to join the lecturing staff. During that period, he produced *Introduction to Islam*, a self-teaching manual on Islam and a *Basic Arabic* with Cassettes. It was during this time he wrote his Recollections and Reflections entitled *Do You Remember …?* Finished in 1988, my copy has "Octogenerian" added in his own handwriting. It is a work of instruction, insight, wisdom, humour, and commitment, with added historical value of "how it was" all those years ago, humbly presented.

John Wood
2017

Acknowledgements

This project would not have succeeded without the help and assistance of a number of people whom we want to acknowledge and honour. Our most grateful appreciation goes to John Wood who alerted us to the existence of Aubrey Whitehouse's manuscript. John has also informed the Arthur Jeffery Centre for the Study of Islam, Melbourne School of Theology of (and in some cases supplied us with) copies of other works by Aubrey. Thank you, John.

We are also very grateful to Richard Coombs, the Director of Middle East Christian Outreach here in Australia who has not only spent time answering emails and searching for information about Aubrey Whitehouse, but has also given the Melbourne School of Theology Press, through the Arthur Jeffery Centre for the Study of Islam, the permission to proceed with publishing materials written by Aubrey.

For the picture of Aubrey and his wife Elsie we are indebted to Annette Cook, the Finance and Administration Manager at MECO for allowing MST Press to copy family photos of Aubrey and his wife taken at their 50th Wedding Anniversary. Since photos of Aubrey and his wife have been hard to obtain we are very grateful for these. The photographs of aspects of the work in Egypt have been taken from a booklet entitled *The Complete Circle: A story of Medical Work in Egypt,* written by A.H. Whitehouse sometime about 1948.

Thanks, too, to Abdou and Judy Grace, Doug and Dulcie Anderson, and Lester Williams, for your contributions – all have been gratefully received.

Ruth Nicholls
Editor

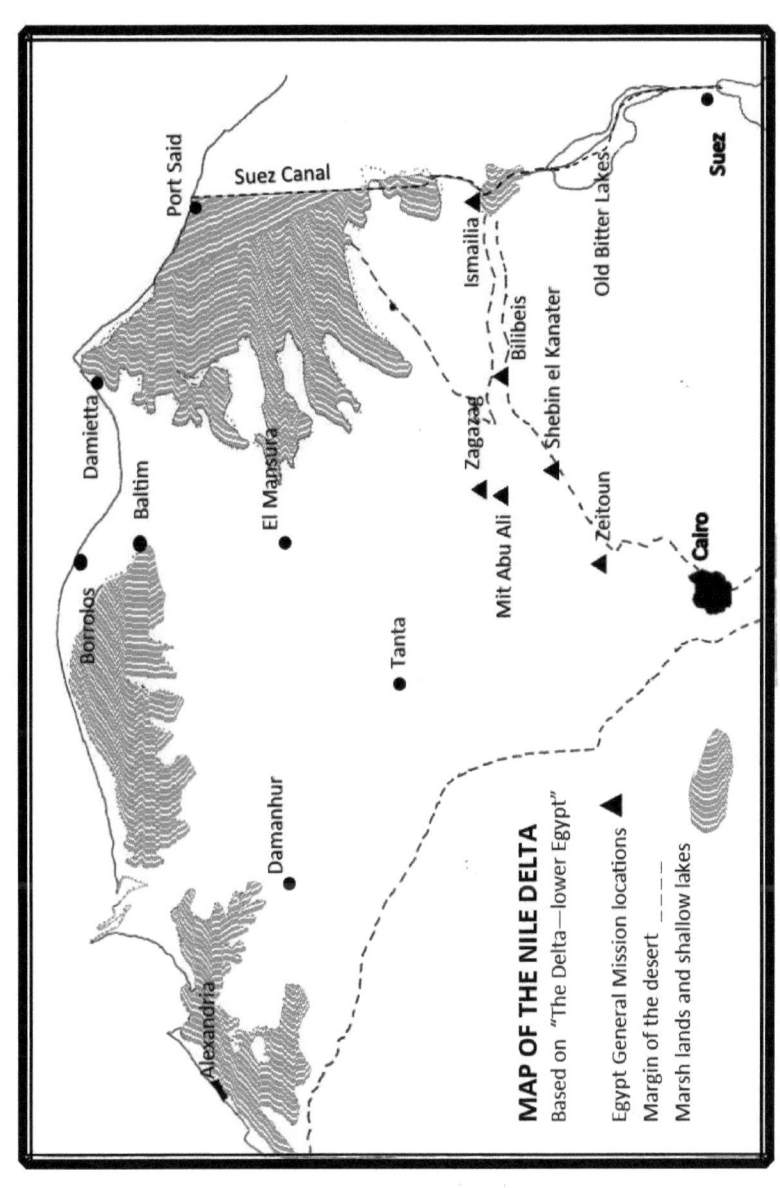

Egypt General Mission Centres

By Way of Explanation

For some time, Lester Williams has been insisting that I should write down some memoirs of my time in Egypt. I have been just as insistent that I had no intention of writing anything like a biography which would be neither interesting, informative nor edifying.

However, at length, as I thought over the matter, I concluded that there could be some interest in recalling some of the experiences we shared in those years. This has been done in the form of correspondence with a close contemporary of mine during the last 21 years of EGM's service in Egypt.

I had hoped that my friend Alan Tucker would perhaps share in the effort, but he felt, rightly I see now, that it would be better for one person to do the job and that his part would be to read, confirm (or amend) and suggest things that might be recorded. This is what we have done.

Under the title of 'Do You Remember...?' I have written to him recalling various experiences, and he has read – and re-read – them. In his last letter to me he wrote – "I recall so much of what you have written and vouch for its truthfulness." So at least as far as we are concerned the record stands, always provided of course that our memories have not betrayed us. After all, we are both in our eighties now.

I don't know what Lester will do with these scribblings. They will no doubt interest the dwindling numbers of those who shared these times with us, but who else? That's up to Lester.

There are many other experiences we reminded each other of as I wrote, but they are mostly little 'private' incidents that just concern us and our immediate close circle of friends. So they are left out. Now, Lester, it's over to you.

Aubrey Whitehouse
Melbourne, 1988.

Junior Missionaries – Language Studies and Related Matters

Since we have retired, I have been involved, almost annually, in orientation seminars for our own new missionaries and those of other societies. These seminars usually last from ten days to a fortnight, or sometimes even longer. How fortunate new missionaries are these days! Looking back on our experience fifty years ago, our "orientation" was very much a matter of being pushed into the deep end; learning most of what we had to learn by trial and error, with considerable emphasis on error. We were very much the "junior missionaries" in those days, and there was quite a gap between "juniors" and "seniors". Thank God for those who bridged the gap and helped us newcomers from down under get adjusted to the norms and mores of a very conservative (or so it seemed to us) British-oriented mission.

Everyone was addressed as Mr, Mrs or Miss, and I remember the shocked reaction of some of our senior missionaries when we began to call our lady contemporaries by their Christian names. That period of two-years probation, before being allowed to marry – and no missionaries came out married in those days – was pretty rigidly enforced, you remember. In addition to that, during the period of engagement we were not allowed to be on the same station or to see each other except at specified intervals. Do you remember Noel's famous remark to the Field Secretary who reproved him for seeing Doreen most Saturdays – "Saturday's my day, Mr. King"!

I remember too, being at Suez with Arthur Skeels when he became engaged to Leida. Leida was then at Zagazig, a distance of two to three hours from Suez (travelling as we did on Egyptian railways). He announced his intention of visiting her by sending a telegram, just simply stating – "Philemon 22 Love Arthur." (*Please keep a guest room ready for me, for I am hoping that God will answer your prayers and let me return to you soon.*) Unfortunately, the telegram landed on the senior missionary's desk instead of Leida's and he was not amused at the cheek of a junior missionary 'ordering' him to prepare a guest room for him.

Speaking of Arthur. You remember he was a 'brother'? I remember one Sunday afternoon we had been visiting British soldiers in the military hospital by the Citadel. This was one of our evangelistic outlets while we were language students and still relatively weak at Arabic. I remember Arthur inviting us one afternoon to a meeting of a Brethren Assembly. We only had small pocket testaments with us, and do you remember how conspicuous we felt (you and I, that is) – when we were invited to sit at the front among the elders with their very large Bibles? To crown the confusion, one of the Elders welcomed 'Brother' Tucker, 'Brother' Whitehouse and 'Mr. Skeels' (the only 'brother' of the three of us), who had been relegated to a back seat.

Of course, we were greatly privileged at being introduced to Arabic and Muslim culture at the School of Oriental Studies (SOS) at the American University. We used to ride on our bikes from EGM Field HQ at Zeitoun to the SOS in Cairo. I think it took us about half an hour or so along Cairo's main streets. Imagine trying to do that now! Do you remember the occasion when there was a special procession for King Farouk, (then a very popular and newly-married), and white-gloved policemen lined all the streets? Jocelyn Cobb, you and I were riding abreast with Jocelyn nearest the line of policemen. I remember suddenly missing Jocelyn, and seeing him, bike and policeman on the ground as Jocelyn, engrossed in conversation, had collided with the policeman. But what I still remember is the policeman, getting up, dusting himself down and saluting Jocelyn. That wouldn't happen now either.

I remember with gratitude those who taught us Arabic Dr. Elder, Dr. Arthur Jeffery, Dr. Enderlein, as well as Atallah Athanasius, Milad Effendi, Sheikhs Sayyid, Zaki, Ahmad, Aziz and others. What a privilege was ours!

Dear old Dr. Enderlein, our German professor was quite a character you remember. Do you remember his chuckle and the way he ended sentences with "So-so-so"? I recall the time when you produced *ragagil* as the plural for *ragil* (man). I can hear his chuckle as he said, "So, you have invented a new word, isn't it? So, you will take the prize isn't it? So-so-so."

I remember too when he was taking a group of us on a visit to the al Azhar mosque and I asked him if it would be appropriate to take a camera. "O no," he said "but if you have a little one that they can't see – So-so-so". He was interned as an enemy alien during the war – not that he would have been any sort of a threat to anyone. Did you ever hear what happened to him afterwards?

And who could forget Arthur Jeffery's inimitable style of teaching and his interspersed anecdotes? But above all I remember his mastery of who knows how many Semitic languages, and how he used the parallel between Hebrew, Aramaic and Arabic to emphasise a point – sometimes to jolt our understanding of Biblical texts. Were you there on that occasion when he was explaining the difficulty of designating definitive meanings to words when there are no diacritical dots on the letters as is the case of early Semitic texts? He noted that we have accepted that Elijah was fed by ravens (*gharab*), during the drought in Israel. However, if the important dots were removed, the word could just as easily and correctly be read as 'Arab' – '*desert Arabs*'. When a fellow student objected that such an interpretation removed the miraculous from the scripture, he replied, "Dear Lady, if desert Arabs daily fed a Jew, that would be a considerable miracle!"

And I have always appreciated the new light that was shed for me on the parable of the Ten Virgins, during our discussions of Arabic plurals. He referred to the Arabic plural for 'young men' (*shabiba*) which, though feminine in form, is masculine in meaning. There are a few such words commonly used in Arabic, as you know. His argument ran something like this – there is a strong possibility that our Lord's discourses to the people were spoken in Aramaic and that the first draft of Matthew's Gospel was also in Aramaic, a sister language to Arabic. He suggested that this Arabic word for 'young men' *(shabiba)* has a similar form in Aramaic. That is, it is feminine in form but masculine in meaning, and it was this word that the Lord probably used to indicate that there were ten young men who went out to meet the bridegroom. When Matthew's gospel was later translated into its present Greek form, the translators translated this masculine plural (with a feminine form) into a feminine Greek word – *parthenos*. Hence, all future translations from the Greek have transformed these young unmarried men into unmarried girls. The irony of it is that when the Greek is translated back into another Semitic language, Arabic, it is translated as a distinctly feminine 'virgin'. For language students, this example provides a lovely exercise in feminine plurals, which are quite complicated in Arabic.

Since hearing this explanation from Arthur Jeffery and becoming familiar with Arab (Egyptian) marriage customs in the villages, I have often wondered, in retrospect, what our Muslim hearers thought when we told them this story, as we often did in the wards of the hospital at Shebin. I wonder too, if the Lord had told this story as the Greek version records it, how His audience would have reacted? His parables were always true to life but this parable, as now recorded, seems contrary to accepted norms of behaviour in today's Middle East, let alone that of the first century.

It would not be 'done' for a group of unmarried girls to go out unchaperoned at midnight to meet a group of men under any circumstances. However, this is how we tell our Arab audiences it happened. As a matter of fact, as you remember, this is not what happens in the villages of Egypt (when we were there at any rate, and no doubt still happens there and in other Middle Eastern countries). What happens in a wedding in the villages is that the young men, the friends of the bridegroom, go out after sunset with lanterns to accompany the bridegroom to the bride's house. I've never seen Arthur Jeffery's perspective published anywhere, but it has always made sense to me.

Speaking of this parable, I remember an Egyptian evangelist who visited us at Shebin at one time (I forget his name), who, also had the habit of finishing just about every sentence with *Ja'ni e:h?* (ie. What does that mean?) It was probably a catechumenal device of his for teaching illiterates Bible truths ... or simply a rhetorical question. On one occasion, he was telling the story of the Ten Virgins to a ward full of men at Shebin hospital and started off with – *kan fi 'ashara binat – ja'ni e:h?* (There were ten girls – what does that mean?) Promptly there was a response from one of the Muslim patients – *harem*.[1]

Looking back on our early efforts with Arabic – and even some not so early efforts – we all had our share of 'howlers'. A lot of them were due to our not differentiating between the various

---

[1] A *harem* can refer to the wives and concubines of one Muslim man or it can refer to the portion of a house which is the women's section.

'heavy' letters and the lighter ones with more or less the same sound.

An Egyptian believer sharing the Good News in outpatients

I recall one occasion, long after my official student days when I was preaching in the church at Shebin. I was very earnestly trying to emphasise the peril the church was in because it was deaf to what God was saying, and I repeated more than once – 'Our trouble, the trouble of the church, is that it is deaf.' Instead of this having a sobering effect on the congregation, I noticed some of the men politely trying to suppress a smile and some of the girl nurses quietly giggling. After the service, I asked Sitt Hayat about the reactions. She was reluctant to tell me, but finally told me that my diagnosis of the ills of the church was that it was pickled! (Maybe I wasn't too far out, though that was not what I intended). On this occasion, it was not a heavy letter that tripped me up, but my failure to pronounce the final *hamza* (glottal stop) clearly. Instead of the feminine *tarsha,* I had used the feminine <u>ending</u> *tarsha.* Is your Arabic still good enough to pick that up?

I remember my fellow students in our language study class urging the Field Council to allow us to live with an Egyptian family for a while to acquire a more fluent use of the language. However, mindful of the fact that 'Borden of Yale', a promising CIM[2] missionary studying Arabic in Cairo, and living with an Egyptian family, had recently contracted typhoid and died, the Council

---

[2] CIM stands for China Inland Mission which later became the Overseas Missionary Fellowship.

refused for a long time to even consider our request. Eventually they agreed to it, but by this time, I had already been appointed to Shebin. But you and Noel each had a spell with Sheikh Azis and family, didn't you? I believe that your pronunciation was more accurate than mine because of that.

I wonder if you found, as I did, that some familiar passages of scripture came alive with new meaning when I read and memorized them in Arabic. In particular, John 14, Phil 2 and Isaiah 3 meant, and I think still mean, much more to me in Arabic than they do in English. Do you think it's just the magic of the Arabic language? Islam of course forbids all forms of magic but the magic of the language, and certainly the recital of the Qur'an in Arabic has an almost hypnotic effect on Arabic-speaking listeners, as you know. I don't think the mere silent reading of the Qur'an affects Muslims in the same way. I have always been glad that our Muslim Sheikhs who guided our reading and conversation at SOS taught us to recite the Qur'an as rhythmically as they did. No doubt you found, as I did, that if it ever became necessary to quote the Qur'an in our contacts with Muslims, our ability to 'chant' it gave us much more acceptance. I found that out later in Eritrea, too. And I remember how pleased I was to find out that the rhythm of Daniel 4:35b in Arabic could be made to sound just like the Qur'an. I often used to quote it in this way when I wanted to emphasize God's sovereignty, rather than quote the Qur'an. And most listeners thought I was quoting from the Qur'an. Do you think that wasn't quite fair?

Since retiring, I have had the opportunity to do further study of Islam, and I was impressed with this quote from J. Laffin ("The Arab Mind" – 1975) which confirms much of my own experience. Did you find the same thing? – "The phonetic beauty of the Arabic language and the musicality of its words invite emotional response and weaken the faculty of reasoning." I wouldn't want to deliberately weaken the faculty of reasoning. On the contrary, I'm sure the Directors of SOS were right in giving us Muslim sheikhs to guide our Arabic studies.

Speaking of this quality of Arabic, I remember years later, a believer from a Muslim background, Sheikh Nur id Din who had been a leading Imam and had an excellent voice in chanting the Qur'an. After his conversion, he worked for some time with ELWA in Beirut with Bud Acord whom you will remember from

Asaab in Eritrea and Aden. He had a special programme in which he chanted the Arabic scriptures as he would the Qur'an. It was a very effective programme and elicited a large response. Bud told me that at some point, they received a letter from a Muslim listener asking what sura of the Qur'an Sheikh Nur id Din had recited, as he did not recognize it.

I think the fact that the Arabic scriptures so readily lend themselves to rhythmical chanting is due to the fact when Van Dyke translated the scriptures into Arabic in the 1860's he had the services of an Azhary Sheikh (for which some criticized him) to produce a high quality but readily understood Arabic. Granted that some of the Arabic words and expressions used in that translation have changed their meaning over the years and need to be revised, I do not feel at home with the present TAV (Today's Arabic Version). I feel sure it has lost a good deal of its appeal to Muslim readers. They do not like tampering with the accepted text of scripture. It only confirms the Qur'anic claim that Christians have altered and corrupted the original scriptures.

I believe that the practice adopted in some non-Arabic-speaking Muslim countries of publishing the Scriptures in a bi-lingual version has much (apart from its cost) to commend it. This reflects the Muslim practice with translations of the Qur'an. Muslims print the original, untranslatable, unalterable Arabic text of the Qur'an in one column (<u>this</u> is the Qur'an) and in a parallel column, an 'interpretation' (translation) of the Qur'an. The Christian equivalent is to print the text of the Greek originals of the New Testament in one column and the translation in a parallel column. It doesn't matter that no-one reads the originals, any more than non-Arabic-speaking people do not read the Arabic column of the Qur'an. Simply, it also provides the original, uncorrupted text of our scriptures available for verifying by anyone who can read it. One of the values of this is that the Greek text as we have it today, ante-dates the Qur'an by at least two centuries and was thus the text which the Qur'an refers to as being "sent down from the Lord of the Worlds" and which the Qur'an in several places professes to confirm. There could be some advantage in doing this with the Arabic scriptures too.

This calls to mind the vast amount of time that Mr George Swan and the Bible Society spent in producing an Egyptian Colloquial version of the scriptures. The rationale behind it was sound, but I never felt very confident in using it. For one thing, colloquial Arabic is a spoken, not a written language and the attempt to represent it in Arabic script without vowels does not make for easy reading. Many a time in an Egyptian village, I would give someone who could read Arabic a copy of a colloquial gospel and ask him to read it to the men gathered around. Invariably he would stumble over words and mispronounce them or have a couple of goes at it, with the result that it was far from being a simplification of the text. I found it much easier to read the classical text and to explain it where necessary in colloquial. I distributed a lot of colloquial scriptures, because they were there and in deference to Mr Swan's years of experience, but I never found that people read them much. I found that if a person could read the colloquial text, he could read the classical and this generally made much more sense to him and was much more like a 'revealed' book than the other. That's just my experience. I wonder what you found?

Talking about Spiritual matters typically occurred outside

At the other extreme from colloquial, I notice the tendency there is today to use Qur'anic terms in the presentation of the Gospel. There is something to be commended in this practice in establishing rapport with Muslims and I have used it myself within limits in verbal discussion with Muslims, but I believe there is a danger in using it on the printed page. In a face-to-face discussion one is interpreting in any case, but when it is printed it tends to be regarded as part of the text of the Gospel, which is something different. Most of the terms used in the Arabic scriptures are intelligible to a Muslim and those which are not are easily explained. But to change the words of the Gospel and to substitute distinctively Qur'anic words is another matter.

Have you seen a recent 'harmony' of the Gospels under the title of "The Life of Christ in a Classical Arabic Tongue"? Commendable is the intention of the compiler and the Arabic and the manner of presentation is lovely. However, this accommodation of Gospel vocabulary to Qur'anic interpretation is carried to extremes, in my personal opinion.

For example, the disciples are referred to by the Qur'anic term *hawariyyin*, whereas the scriptural term *talamiz* is perfectly well understood and conveys the meaning of disciples much more accurately. Similarly, in Christ's trial before Caiaphas, the High Priest, is referred to as *al Mufti* and he asks Christ if He is *al Mahdi*, to which Christ assents. Apart from the fact that this is an anachronism, the words are purely Qur'anic and unnecessary as Christ is regularly referred to in the Qur'an as *al Mesih* (the Messiah). So why the alteration?

Worse, in my judgement, is the way the compiler of the "Life of Christ" puts the words of the Islamic call to prayer on the lips of the Lord when, in Gethsemane, He found the disciples sleeping. He is reported as saying *Prayer is better than sleep, so awake to prayer*. Every Muslim would recognise that as part of the Muslim call to prayer in the early morning, and in any case, it misrepresents what the Lord said.

A final word on scripture translation. There are a lot of things I like about the Good News Bible, and I use it for my evening devotion, but I wish the translators had left the word *leprosy* in the text and simply made a footnote, (as does the NIV) explaining that the Greek word was used for various diseases, not necessarily leprosy. Instead they consistently translate the word by a clumsy phrase: *a dreaded skin disease*. This lands them in a difficulty when they come to translate *the house of Simon the Leper* in Mark 14:3. We get the phrase, for which there is no justification in the text – Simon, *a man who had suffered from a dreaded skin disease*.

If they had lived in the Middle East, they would have realised that the words *the Leper* had nothing to do with his health, but was simply a family name. The popular Arab singer, al Atrash is certainly not deaf, as his name would be translated, nor did our Egyptian friend 'Aryan Butros (naked Peter) run around naked. One of the leading Evangelical pastors in Lebanon is named Selim Sihyuni (Selim, the Zionist). I asked him once if his name ever landed him in trouble and he said, "Not the least. Everyone knows it's my family name".

On this same subject, I believe the same applies to Simon the Tanner with whom Peter stayed in Joppa. Peter at this time still had very real scruples about ceremonial uncleanness, as the story itself illustrates, and would hardly have chosen to stay with someone engaged in the trade of tanning. It is much more likely that *The Tanner* was Simon's family name or moniker. As a matter of fact, Simon was such a common name that in wording a record such as the Gospels or Acts, it was necessary to distinguish which Simon was meant, hence the use of the moniker.

I suppose, come to that, that our Anglo-Saxon names could be treated the same way. No one translating my name into Arabic would describe me as 'Aubrey, the man who lived in the White House', nor for that matter would they translate your name as 'Alan, the Gourmet!'[3] So, so, so – as Dr. Enderlein would have said.

---

[3] In colloquial Australian, 'tucker' can refer to food or a meal.

Fellow-Workers

I remember hearing of the missionary to a pagan[4] country who was once asked what his greatest problems were. He answered – first, myself, second my fellow workers, and third the pagans. I guess that order is more or less valid wherever we happen to serve. It reminds me of that other little ditty:

> *To dwell above with saints we love*
> *that will be greatest glory.*
> *To dwell below with saints we know –*
> *Ah, that's a different story.*

I suppose both observations apply much more to single missionaries than to married couples. And as we all in our day went out single and remained that way for at least two years during our probationary period, we had some experience of it.

The root of the problem is compatibility. While in our Home countries one does not, as a rule, have to live with the people with whom one works (unless you're down in the Antarctic) the mission situation as we knew it was quite different. If you were a single missionary, you couldn't get away from those with whom you worked, day or night. In many cases that worked out quite satisfactorily, but in others, it didn't. If a person who was very meticulous and to whom appointments and punctuality were important, was teamed with someone of a contemplative nature who considered relating to people was most important even if it meant being late for something else, there could be tensions and problems.

This problem of compatibility, remember, occupied us sometimes for hours at a Field Council meeting when a vacancy in one centre meant a re-shuffle of personnel on several others. How many times what seemed as a neat solution was torpedoed by a lady

---

[4] In this day, this would not be considered a politically correct term though it was a word that would have been frequently used when Whitehouse was writing.

council member saying, "You can't put those two together. They will never get on." Then we'd have to start all over again. Sometimes the process extended over two or three council meetings if it wasn't too urgent, because of our principle of never appointing anyone, except a probationer, without consultation with all the parties concerned.

The situation was often most acute when it concerned young missionaries – 'junior missionaries' in the terminology of those days. Young people coming out with fresh ideas and enthusiasm often found themselves stationed with senior missionaries who appeared to be very conservative and conscious of the status quo. That had the potentiality for misunderstandings and difficulties for both parties. There were notable exceptions. Do you remember Kath Channing? What a delightful soul she was, deeply spiritual but also very practical and understanding. What a gift she was to the Field Council when it came to locating a difficult person. Appoint her to be with Kath! I never remember anyone who couldn't get on with Kath and I am sure there were a number of lady missionaries who often had occasion to thank God for her wise and loving understanding of their problems while they were stationed with her.

Of course, there were many occasions when people who were thrown together clicked immediately; forming deep and lasting friendships. I can think of several. Think of Kathleen Smythe and Alex Liblik for instance. Although there was quite a gap in their ages and they were from different countries, they got on marvellously together and one could never think of the one without the other.

Incidentally, do you remember the lovely story about Kathleen, Alex and Phoebe? I only have it second-hand from you and Noel; it also may have been embellished with the passing of the years. They had acquired a car at a time when cars were a rarity in the mission (The Tel-el-Kebir ladies were still driving around in a horse and buggy). They called the car 'Phoebe' – the servant of the church. The difficulty was that whenever they referred to the car in their prayer newsletters they referred to it as though it were a person and you and Noel and Arthur, then students at BTI, NZ, and very interested in Egypt, thought it was a Bible Woman. You prayed most fervently for Phoebe, especially after she had had a breakdown. However, when it was reported that she had had a blow-out, some suspicions were aroused. When at length the news was that Phoebe had busted her big end, you were completely disillusioned. Have I got the story right? It's a good story anyway.

A car was an aid to village ministry

Alex Liblik was an Estonian and I am reminded of other Estonian missionaries, especially dear Dr Melita Marley, a most gracious and lovely Christian character. The saying is 'it is more blessed to give than to receive' and I am sure that on the whole, giving is easier too. Melita was the one person above all that I knew, who could most graciously receive. She has meant a lot to Elsie and me and still does, and as for the thousands of Egyptians she treated, the influence on them of her life and her medical skills may never be known. Like all our Estonian missionaries, she spoke excellent English with only an occasional mannerism to betray her. Do you remember the medical report she wrote on Elsie one year? We had to have an annual check-up you remember. Elsie had had quite a lot of mishaps and illnesses during the year which Melita listed and then finished her report with "apart from that she has had excellent health."

And what about Esther, another Estonian? She was probably one of the best linguists (among other things), we had in the Mission. But even she got infected with the English used by some of the troops from NZ and UK during the war when we entertained so many of them at the hospital. At that time, I remember her praying at one of our staff prayer meetings in very precise English for "that bloke in bed in the men's ward." Esther was brilliant in many ways and an exceptionally hard worker. I guess that made it a little difficult for some who were later stationed with her in

Eritrea. She was the first of our contemporaries to pass over to the other side. I remember Lois Thornton writing to me at that time and making the remark – "Esther has beaten us all to glory."

Were you ever stationed with 'Pills' and 'Bobby' Ward during your single days? I lived with them for quite a time. One of my problems was getting enough to eat. Bobby had great ideas of colour schemes for meals. I can't recall just now what colours went with what, but in any case, our staple vegetable in Egypt was *kusa* (a small marrow) which was generally pretty nondescript in colour by the time it reached the table. That wasn't my problem though. It was that they both had small appetites and I had quite a healthy appetite and found some difficulty in satisfying it. Bobby used to make soda bread – terribly heavy stuff, but I filled up on it. I found out afterwards that she told one or the other missionaries on the compound that "Aubrey likes my soda bread, he eats so much of it."

That brings me to the subject of marriage and weddings. In those days, transport abroad was of course by ship and fairly slow by today's standards. That meant that very few of us indeed could either get home for a wedding or have their folk come out to Egypt for it. So what usually happened was that the Field Leader and his wife acted as 'parents'. George Swan, one of the founders of EGM, and his wife acted for Elsie and myself, and later you yourself acted in this capacity for various other couples.

Things didn't go very smoothly for Elsie and myself. We had planned our wedding for June 20th, 1940 and arranged, in the usual way, to have the official consular wedding in the morning and the church service in the afternoon. Also in the usual way, Elsie and I were separated by the Mission prior to the wedding. Elsie was at HQ in Zeitoun and I was 20 miles away at Shebin.

On the morning of 12th June, I had a call from the Consul-General. If I intended getting married we would have to come to the consulate right away as, due to the proximity of the advancing Italian forces to Cairo, the Embassy was packing up and preparing to leave. I was unable to contact our HQ in Zeitoun to alert Elsie, but I requisitioned the hospital car and rushed off to Zeitoun. Neither Elsie nor the Swans were able to get dressed up, but I bundled them all into the car as they were and got to the consulate just in time. With typical British phlegm, the Consul-General walked into the courtroom wearing a monocle as though thoughts of evacuation were miles away. As we stood before him he looked down at the documents on the table before him, looked up at Elsie and said, "Many Happy Returns". We thought, "What a strange thing to say at a wedding", and then we realized that in our hurry to get married we had momentarily forgotten it was Elsie's birthday.

We had the church service as planned 8 days later, and in the meantime, Elsie went back with Mr & Mrs. Swan and I went back to Shebin. Mr Swan, whom you remember was always very 'correct' was in a bit of a dilemma as to how to address Elsie in the interregnum. He couldn't call her "Miss Percy" any more, so he settled for "Mrs Aubrey". Our personal dilemma was to know which day was our wedding anniversary. For some time, we celebrated the 20th June, but finally decided it was more sensible to celebrate the date on our marriage certificate, which is Elsie's birthday. So we have celebrated the two together ever since.

Speaking of mission weddings, I remember when Harry Young (then with LEM) was married to a girl from TEAM. The wedding was at Beirut during the mini civil war in 1958 and Harry wanted the service entirely in Arabic. The problem was that Raymond Joyce, the Field Leader of TEAM at the time, who was to give the bride away, did not know any Arabic, so they fixed up a cue for him. When the officiating minister asked a question ("Who gives this woman away..."), he would pause, look at Raymond who would then say *Ana* (I do). So Raymond was up front waiting for his cue. Then when the minister asked if anyone objected to these two being joined in lawful matrimony, he paused in the usual way and looked around the congregation.

Raymond, thinking this was his cue, responded loudly and clearly – *Ana*. There was a slight embarrassed pause, but I don't think very many in the congregation heard the gaffe as by then there was a lot of heavy firing going on around the place and, as a matter of fact, by the time the ceremony was over, quite a number of the congregation had already disappeared heading for home.

But back to Egypt. By and large, I think the EGM family was a very happy family. One person who stands out in my memory was Herbert 'Paddy' Mercer, but I don't think anyone ever called him 'Herbert', not even his wife. Paddy was a man of prayer. It's as that I mostly remember him. Paddy was on very intimate terms with the Lord, with a great concern for His honour and glory. Do you remember the occasion when we were very short of finance and you, as the Field Secretary at the time, called us together for a time of special prayer? Elsie and I were seconded to the Nile Mission Press at Zeitoun just then, so we joined in with the HQ group. Paddy too, was based on Zeitoun and came bustling in to the sitting room where we were gathered, just as we were about to start the meeting. In his haste, he grabbed hold of the door handle and gave it a sharp pull, and it came away in his hand. He was quite upset about it and I remember your saying to him, "That's just the reason we're gathered Paddy. We're so short of finance we can't keep our buildings in repair." I don't remember what Paddy said to that, but I do remember his prayer a few minutes later. He said something like this –

> "Lord, we've come together to pray for money and they tell us we haven't got enough money to keep our buildings in repair. When you come into a room Lord, and grab the door handle, it comes off in your hand, Lord. It's a disgrace to your work, Lord."

Paddy always felt that the Lord's work should be fully funded. In fact, I remember that he did not agree when we praised the Lord for a three quarter's or seven-eighth's allowance. He reckoned it should always be full. Anything less reflected on the Lord's ability to provide for His work and workers.

I remember that earlier occasion when some of us junior missionaries – seven of us, bachelors – gathered for a weekend of prayer at Belibeis. Although Paddy was several years our senior in age and 'status', we asked him to join us for the sheer inspiration of his prayers. Neither Paddy nor we were conscious of any generation gap. And I remember him praying – "we're just a bunch of young fellers Lord..." But I'm thinking particularly about one session of prayer when we were conscious of our lack of enthusiasm and boldness in witness, when Paddy took up the theme –

> "Lord, these Muslim sheikhs put us to shame. When you're travelling in a third-class carriage, Lord and the time for prayer comes, these Muslim fellows will get up and push you off the seat Lord, so that they can say their prayers."

This vivid word picture set the rest of us off laughing and eventually Paddy joined in. Then he apologised to the Lord – "We're laughing Lord, but its holy laughter, Lord."

Paddy, you remember, was in charge of our colportage work and he was an indefatigable distributor of the scriptures. I remember how upset he was with me once: I told him that I gave away scores of the gospels to patients going home from hospital and to ex-patients we visited in their villages. He told me I should sell them, not give them away. "But these people are our friends," I remonstrated. "They're *just* the people you should sell to," he rejoined. I think Paddy was more correct than I. People will always value what they pay for, even if it is only a nominal sum, much more than something given away. And perhaps they feel we don't value our scriptures very highly if we distribute them freely. On the other hand, of course, if they don't want to pay even a nominal sum, feeling that hospitality demands a gift, what do you do?

Going back to the matter of the gap which existed to a certain extent between junior and senior missionaries, I remember at that time – in the thirties – there was also a distinct gap between the missionaries and national (paid) workers, particularly servants, cleaners, door-keepers and so forth. At that time, the latter group were referred to as 'Native workers' – a term which I suppose is etymologically correct, but which always seemed to me to have a derogatory connotation. We had not then progressed to referring to 'expatriate' and 'national' workers. This always upset me quite a bit having come from an egalitarian Australian society, as did the fact that when I happened to pass a group of 'natives' sitting on a bench, they would stand up as I came along. I was so upset about it that I preached on the subject at one of our regular staff services on Sunday evenings. Taking Col 3:11 as my text, I transformed Paul's words into "missionaries and natives, Egyptians and foreigners..." etc. I remember, in my brashness suggesting we should call our 'native workers', 'Egyptian fellow workers'. My temerity received more publicity than I had intended. A few weeks later I was having lunch with Norman and Pat Anderson, when Pat, with a twinkle passed me some *balady* (native) bread and said, "Have some Egyptian fellow-worker bread, Aubrey."

While on this subject, you remember that in our village churches we had followed the custom of the country of having a screen down the middle of the church dividing the men on the right from the women on the left. 'Pills' and I had long discussions about the practice and eventually brought up the subject at one of our staff meetings. We argued that scripturally there was no justification for it. On the contrary, in Christ there is neither male nor female and we should not put a barrier between them. There was quite a lot of opposition to the idea, but at length it was decided to give it a try.

If I remember rightly, we had our Egyptian workers – who formed most of the congregation – vote on it, and there was sufficient support to enable us to dismantle it. However, the rear-guard of the opposition were not happy and reckoned this went for most if not all of the womenfolk. So, we had another vote and this time, by the narrowest of margins, it was decided to put it back. 'Pills' was very upset with me for giving in to the decision as he reckoned the vote was 'rigged'. He was so upset that he vowed to never attend any meetings in the church while the screen was there. I think it was during the war that it was finally removed.

I suppose this topic raises the whole question of interpretation of scripture in matters concerning the culture and customs of the people. In the early church, in cities there were no screens and husbands and wives normally sat together, but country churches were influenced no doubt by the dominant presence of Islam and most Coptic Orthodox churches. 'Pills' and I contended that Christian attitudes should not be determined by Islam, particularly in customs of *harem,* but I'm not altogether sure now that that was the issue. The fact is that centuries of conforming to the prevailing custom – if that was what it was – had virtually made it a Christian custom too.

Since we who raised the matter were men, it could easily be misinterpreted that we would be deflected from our worship of God by observing the female section of the congregation and vice versa. I was a single man at the time which made it more reprehensible to some minds. At the same time, screen or no screen, when I preached from the pulpit I could see and be seen by both men and women. However, we did observe very rigorously the division of the sexes in that I never spoke to women except *en masse* and the lady missionaries as a rule, left the men to the men.

Looking back, I think we young missionaries from down under were rather too iconoclastic. We were probably precipitate in attempting to abolish a custom which, while objectionable to us, did not do much, if anything, to hinder the worship of the Lord in Spirit and in Truth.

While thinking of our fellow-workers, we must not overlook our Egyptian fellow-workers. How much we depended on them and how much we owed them.

Remember Saad Mansur? What a testimony he was to the value of one-on-one interaction. It was Archie Hay, wasn't it, who spent days and weeks – indeed months – in personal instruction and fellowship with Saad. And we who followed on entered into that inheritance. Saad was eloquent in the scriptures with a wide understanding of Islam and a great zeal for evangelism. What a privilege it was to work together with him!

Do you remember the time when you and I were stationed together at Belibeis while Hammie and Susan were on furlough? We were then doing advanced Arabic studies, but were still glad to leave most of the preaching to Saad. Do you remember market days at Belibeis? Our compound faced the dusty road that led to the market place and on market days, literally thousands of people came past our door. We had a hefty door opening on to the road which led to a large waiting room for the clinic. We would open this door and leave Saad to preach to the people who came in. Our part was mainly out in the street urging people to go in – 'Free water and free seats' was part of our line.

Do you remember one occasion when the room was full and we were still outside urging people in, when we sensed things weren't going too well? When we came back to the room, *there* was Saad standing up on a table with a menacing crowd led by a Sheikh milling around him. It looked quite grim. Now we – you and I – had the reverse task of getting all the people out without a riot. When we had finally cleared the room, and locked and bolted the door, Saad came down from the table. In his best dictionary English, he informed us that "that Sheikh was willing to strike me." More than willing, we thought.

Do you remember the consternation on the face of one of the UK soldiers who visited us during the war, who, to make conversation asked Saad where he lived? Now Saad knew from the dictionary that the outer fringes of a town were called the outskirts, but he lived within the town, so he informed the soldier, "I live on the skirts of the town." But these linguistic difficulties worked the other way too. I remember Jocelyn Cobb, always anxious to use his limited Arabic, coming up to Saad on one occasion. Saad had been clean-shaven, but now he sported a slight moustache. Jocelyn did not know the Arabic for 'moustache', so he said, – "That thing under your nose Saad, is it new?"

But it was as an evangelist we most remember him. Do you remember how he preached at funerals? These were great opportunities to preach the gospel to virtually a whole village – the male section of it anyway. A great *maytam* (marquee) would be erected in the village and all the men would go there for three days to sit with the mourners. Usually a well-known Sheikh would be hired to recite the Qur'an. Sometimes more than one.

We would sit there quietly with the others having greeted all the mourners in turn. At length, the Sheikh reciting the Qur'an would pause and come and sit with the mourners. Then Saad would get up and in beautiful Arabic would courteously express his sorrow and sympathy and then naturally and impressively speak of the Christian hope. He was always most attentively listened to. His Arabic was fluent, his arguments simple and sound, and above all, his sincerity was apparent to all. And, of course, the very occasion conditioned the hearers to listen to a message of hope when to them this was the most hopeless of all situations. How much I learned from him. A great deal of any ability I have in relating to Muslims I learned from Saad and from Mousa the believer from a Muslim background who worked with us at Shebin. And we both remember I'm sure, the rich fellowship we enjoyed on our way out to or coming back from a village we had visited for evangelistic ministry.

While on the subject of Saad's beautifully clear and easily understood Arabic, and his extensive knowledge of Islam, together with his experience of meeting and overcoming Islamic problems and objections, this was reflected in that series of teaching tracts that we produced. I'm sure you encountered the same problems as I did in the villages. We had a fairly wide variety of evangelistic tracts which we used extensively, but we had nothing to give to any intelligent Muslim to follow up discussions we may have had on some of the problems that hindered his understanding of the gospel – problems of the reliability of our scriptures, the Trinity, the deity and atoning work of Christ and so forth. We would usually leave him with a gospel – Luke or John – and while no doubt the Holy Spirit does use even the unaccompanied scripture to lead people to Christ, as was the case with Pastor Marcus, usually some explanation of the Muslim's particular problems is necessary. We had nothing of this nature in a compact, readable form which could be used to follow up or consolidate the discussions we had had with such people. And we were very conscious of the fact that we would be unlikely in the normal course of things to meet him again for some time, if ever.

Do you remember we produced that series of twelve doctrinal booklets (about 32 pages if I remember rightly) each one complete in itself, but also part of the series. The idea was to deal with the Muslim's problems understandingly and scripturally, doing so in a way that did not appear to be confrontational (to use the modern phraseology) or an attack on Islam. That would have been self-defeating. So, we produced them with the ostensible – but I think also genuine – purpose of teaching Christians the elements of their faith. At the same time, in doing so we always had the Muslim in mind and sought to answer his objections without raising them. This was where Saad's knowledge of Islam and long experience of working with Muslims was invaluable. I believe these tracts made our village visiting much more effective, but we haven't much way of knowing.

Speaking of tracts, I recall that we made use of the wordless book quite a bit – just four coloured pages, black for the heart of sin, red for the blood of Christ, white for the cleansed heart and gold for glory. This never raised any problems for us in Egypt, but I wonder if missionaries working in Africa ever used the wordless book, and whether, if so, they found any problem in making black synonymous with sin and white with the clean heart. In any case, I don't think the wordless book is scripturally accurate. I have just been checking up and as far as I can see, the Bible never refers to sins as black, but red or crimson. Nor is the sinful heart ever referred to as black. So, the wordless book, as well as being possibly offensive to black people is perhaps not very scriptural either. Incidentally, have you ever looked at a red rose through a red glass?

Thank you for reminding me of that interview with Saad at our Field Council meeting. Saad, like all our Egyptian colleagues received a regular salary, while we missionaries, operating on a 'faith' basis received what was available after all expenses had been met. That meant at that time, that sometimes we might only receive 3/4 or 7/8 allowance, or even less. Saad, who shared so many of our experiences, wanted to share with us financially too and to trust the Lord to supply even when funds were short. We very much appreciated Saad's attitude, but felt that his family circumstances would make living that way difficult, so we asked him to meet with us at our council meeting. We felt that Saad himself could well be prepared to accept the 'faith' principle, but we had doubts about his wife and family. So, we asked him if his wife shared his views on living by faith.

Now there are three *th* sounds in Arabic, one light, one medium and one heavy. However, most Arabic-speaking people (with presumably the exception of the 'Arabs' themselves) find a difficulty in pronouncing this sound and usually replace the lighter *th* sound by an *s* sound and the medium and heavy sounds by a *z* sound. Thus *haithu* is pronounced *haisu* and *thulima* as *zulima*. So, when we asked Saad what was his wife's attitude to the 'faith' principle, he replied, 'Well, really, my wife's face is not like my face.' It took a second or two for the penny to drop, but we felt in the circumstances it would be better for the matter to be held in abeyance for the time being.

There were many other faithful and effective Egyptian fellow workers. Noel would certainly have listed Girgis Effendi, the headmaster of the Boys' school at Ismailia who gave many years of capable and effective service there, and there were some wonderful Bible women who deserve special mention for the way they trusted the Lord and carried on with the witness for years after we as a mission had been expelled from Egypt. And when they were no longer able to engage in active witness in that way, they continued to meet together for prayer.

I never had much to do with the Bible women, naturally, but did have more contact with those who served at the hospital. I am reminded of Sitt Mariam, the sister of one of the leading Evangelical pastors, in charge of the large church in Ezbekiah,

Cairo? She always referred to her brother as THE pastor, you remember, as though there were no other. Brother and sister were both real characters. The pastor had quite a good singing voice – remarkable for an Egyptian – and used to teach the students at the seminary to sing, but he was very short of wind. I remember his leading an Easter service at Shebin once and leading the singing in the Easter hymn. I can still hear him singing "Ha-ha-ha-ha-ha-ha-hallelujah." But he certainly could preach, as indeed most Egyptians could.

Apropos of this, I don't ever remember a trained Egyptian pastor preaching from notes and certainly not reading his sermon. These pastors were well trained in a conservative Presbyterian tradition and their sermons regularly had an introduction, three main points and a conclusion – and of course, as you know, the Arabic language lends itself readily to alliteration. I suppose the influence of trained Muslim orators around them also helped these pastors to memorise their sermons. In any case, Egyptians have phenomenal memories. You remember that boys trained in a Qur'anic village school could often recite the whole of the Qur'an word perfect by the time they were twelve.

Then there were many other faithful fellow-workers who were not gifted speakers but were the kind of people who could be depended on in attending to the practical affairs of the Mission. I think of Sheikh Sidraq. As I was for most of my time in Egypt convenor of the Building Committee, I had a lot to do with him as a handy man, especially in the early years when my Arabic was limited. Sidraq's knowledge of Arabic was good, but his use of it was pretty meagre. His conversation was punctuated with *Ja'ni masalan* – how would you translate that? "That is to say, for instance?" – which did duty for all kinds of expressions which one came to interpret in their context, but which often had very little to do with *ja'ni masalan*. And whenever, something was missing and had to be replaced, he would say *Ja'ni masalan*, "we will make something".

Were you with me when Mr & Mrs King went on furlough and left us in charge of their home and left their little dog with Sidraq? Just before the Kings were due back, the dog died and I remember walking home from church the Sunday before, with Sidraq when he told us with a wry chuckle that the dog had died. "What are you going to do Sidraq?" I asked him. Out came his standard phrase for such occasions: *Ja'ni masalan*, "we will make something."

I was always amazed at the way building workers invariably seemed to understand what it was Sidraq wanted of them. I remember on one occasion he was up a ladder and wanted a hammer. He shouted down to the group of men below *Ya ismak e:h, hat il bita'a* (What's your name, hand me the thingumabob), and promptly one of the men handed him a hammer. All of which makes me wonder that perhaps one's expression and inflexion of voice is as important as vocabulary and syntax when it comes to being understood. You remember the Greek shopkeepers we encountered in the towns and villages in the country? They spoke atrocious Arabic and no one could accuse them of sexist discrimination, for they mixed up masculine and feminine genders as freely as they mixed up everything else. Yet they always seemed to be understood. Perhaps they and Sidraq had something in common that we hadn't cottoned on to.

Sidraq was a faithful, dependable soul, with a deep but simple faith and he was greatly attached to Mr Swan, one of the founders of EGM. I remember at Mr Swan's funeral, he was greatly distressed and not long after, he too went to be with the Lord.

Believers from Muslim backgrounds

I remember how I felt on furlough when one came in contact with missionaries to 'pagan' fields who could talk of hundreds of converts, when we could think only in terms of individuals. Perhaps I'm not sure how I felt – was it embarrassment, or a sense of failure, or was it a subconscious excusing of oneself for lack of 'results' by blaming it on the resistance of Islam? At this distance, I'm not sure. Perhaps underlying it all was a sense of defeat that should not have been. The God who could transform Saul of Tarsus is surely just the same today. On the other hand, of course, the parallel with Saul is perhaps valid, for some of those Muslim Sheikhs who came to Christ were mighty in word and deed.

The late Dr. Charles Malik, a Lebanese scholar and one of the most outstanding Christians in the Middle East, who was one time President of the United Nations, wrote in an article in "Religion in the Middle East" (ed. A.J. Arberry, 1969):

> Conversion from Islam to any form of Christianity is virtually unknown. ... [t]he very few cases of converts from Islam have been most remarkable, alike in the depth of their conviction, in the clarity of their mind as to what it is all about and in the intensity of their love for their fellow man. They have put many born Christians to shame.[5]

As I wrote that I was thinking of some outstanding men and women believers from Muslim backgrounds whom we have known and loved in Egypt. You remember Sheikh Kamal Mansur, Pastor Marcus Abdul Mesih, Sitt Hayat Kamil and others.

Could you ever forget dear old Sheikh Kamal? He was, you remember, a frequent visitor to the hospital at Shebin. I can see him now with a wonderful smile transforming a not very

---

[5] P335, "The Orthodox Church", *Religion in the Middle East,* ed. A. J. Arberry, Cambridge, University Press, 1969.

handsome face, sporting a massive walking stick that looked as though it could be a formidable weapon in an argument, but which I am sure was never used in that way. But you remember what a tower of strength he always was when we had problems with or about believers from Muslim backgrounds. Alongside his wise comments his gentle spirit was a great encouragement and help. He was a very shrewd judge of character and motives too.

I remember on one occasion a fellow came to me and said he wanted to become a Christian – just like that, out of the blue. He didn't know a thing about Christianity, but said he had become disillusioned with Islam. I suspected he thought we might offer him some financial or other help, and it could have been a trap set by the Muslim Brotherhood. Anyhow, it happened that Sheikh Kamal was at Shebin that morning, so I went to him to enlist his help. I introduced Sheikh Kamal to this chap, explaining that he had been a Muslim and had become a Christian. Sheikh Kamal sat down with us and listened to what this 'inquirer' had to say. Then he beamed at him and said something like this – "I understand that you are dissatisfied with Islam and so want to become a Christian. But why do you want to become a Christian specifically! Why don't you become a Jew?" So wise, so shrewd.

We remember Sheikh Kamal as a benign fatherly figure – and he was that to all the believers from Muslim backgrounds – but it was not ever thus. Do you remember the story of his conversion as he told it to us? His brother, Sheikh Mikhail was one of the leading intellectuals of al Azhar. We never knew him because he had gone to glory before we got to Egypt. He had attended discussion meetings which Samuel Zwemer, Temple Gairdner and others had organized with Muslim intellectuals. Eventually, to the great consternation and outrage of his Muslim colleagues, Sheikh Mikhail accepted Christ. When he was baptized, Sheikh Kamal was then still a student at al Azhar. When he heard of it, he went with several other students to where his brother was speaking one night, determined to kill him and wipe out the shame from the family. He told us how he had rushed up to the front of the hall to carry out his intention. When his brother saw him coming he stood there, opened wide his cloak ('exposed his chest' as Sheikh Kamal expressed it) and said – "I'm not afraid or ashamed to die as a Christian. My Master died for me on the cross and I am prepared to die for Him".

Sheikh Kamal told of the effect these words had on him and he felt as though he was being held back from doing anything. He was amazed at the change in his brother's character and decided to find out what had happened. So, the next night he went around to his house. Sheikh Mikhail's wife opened the door and when she saw Kamal she was about to shut the door quickly, fearing that he had come to do harm to his brother. Mikhail had heard his brother's voice and invited him in. The anger had gone from Kamal by this time and he was genuinely anxious to know what had changed his brother. That night he too became a Christian – and what a Christian!

I remember too Pastor Marcus Abdul Mesih, the pastor of the Mission's circuit of Evangelical churches and in particular, pastor of the Evangelical church at Zeitoun. Elsie and I were married there and Pastor Marcus took part in the service. You remember the story of his conversion through reading a portion of scripture he had picked up and the trail that led to his reading of the gospel and his subsequent acceptance of Christ. He was not only a very effective preacher in Egypt, but in later years, he was in much demand in other Middle Eastern countries and even in UK and Europe. Although he had an excellent command of classical Arabic, he made very effective use of colloquialisms especially in illustrations. I can still recall some of these now.

Pastor Marcus's story highlights one of the problems faced by believers from Muslim backgrounds, in those days at any rate – the problem of finding a wife. Suitable women believers from Muslim backgrounds were hard to find, and no Christian was prepared to allow his daughter to marry a believer from a Muslim background for fear he should recant under pressure and go back to his old religion. Marcus faced that problem. Eventually a simple Bible Society colporteur agreed to his marrying his daughter. Although the girl was a believer, she was illiterate and this was always a problem in her taking her full part as a pastor's wife.

And what about Sitt Hayat – a beautiful character – all 20 stone of her. Well, perhaps not quite that, but she was no lightweight, although she carried it with great dignity and graciousness. She was a product of our Girls School at Belbeis, wasn't she? She came from a middle class professional family. Quite uncharacteristically, they never disowned her and always held her in high esteem. I'm sure you have visited her brothers as I have, on quite a few times, and always courteously received.

Her lovely Christian life made a very deep impression on the rest of the family, though none of them made a public profession of faith in Christ. I feel sure that some of them were not far from the kingdom and who knows what may have happened after we left Egypt and she spent the closing years of her life in the old home. Like Sheikh Kamal, Hayat was a great help with women believers from Muslim backgrounds and inquirers with her wealth of experience, her knowledge of the scriptures and depth of spirituality. Elsie kept in touch with her after we were expelled from Egypt, and others of our missionaries, right up to the time of her death.

Then there was Musa Abdul Fadi and his wife Rifqa. I'm sure we didn't appreciate Musa as much as we should have done, but I learned a lot about Islam from him and the approach to Muslims as we went out visiting in the Muslim villages together, and I'm sure you did too. And of course he was our colleague at the Farm Colony. He too, illustrates another problem faced by believers from Muslim backgrounds.

When believers were baptised, especially if they had a very distinctive Muslim name, such as Muhammad or Ali or Fatma, they mostly wished to change their name as part of their testimony to a changed life. Maybe some missionaries suggested a change of name, but I think the initiative mostly came from the believers themselves. The problem arose if the believer wished to register his or her change of name and status from being a Muslim to being a Christian. It was virtually impossible to do so and involved a lot of legal and other procedures. For this reason, I guess, few legally changed their status. Musa was a case in point. As far as the government and local officials were concerned, he did not exist as Musa Abdul Fadi and could only sign legal documents with his old Muslim name. The children of these believers however, could be registered as Christians, so when Musa bought a house, the deeds were in the name of one of his children, not his. I'm not sure, but I expect that when he died (we were not in Egypt at the time) his death certificate would have been made out in his old Muslim name.

The changed name was usually chosen to have some relation to the old name, but at the same time to indicate the change in their life. I suppose Sitt Hayat Kamil illustrates this as well as any. Her Muslim name was 'Aisha', the name of the prophet's favourite wife, which also means 'Life'. Hayat changed it to 'Hayat' which is the word used consistently in the New Testament for eternal life.

One of the problems of names in Arabic of course is that apart from a few which are common to both Islam and Christianity such as Ibrahim (Abraham) and Abdallah (the slave of God), the name is a relatively clear indication of the religion of the person. Do you remember the problem we had in getting a visa for a prominent Christian evangelist from Iran to visit Egypt? In Iran, as a matter of principle, believers from Muslim backgrounds did not change their names and the Egyptian government refused to believe that Rev. Mahmud Resavi, was a Christian minister.

There were other consequences to changing a name too, especially the family name. I suppose that a lot of Muslims in the villages did not so much object to one of their family becoming a Christian per se, as they did to the shame and disgrace it brought on the family, especially if it involved rejecting the family name and choosing another. I think that was probably the thinking behind the attitude adopted by Christians in Iran. On the government level, interestingly, it seems significant that the recent charges brought against those turning from Islam to Christianity recently has been that of 'despising Islam'.

Coming back to Musa and Rifqa, it was from Rifqa that I learned one of the most important lessons I ever learned about preaching to Muslims, at a Christmas service in the Women's wards. She was telling in a very simple and effective way the story of Christ's birth, starting with the annunciation. When she reached the point of the angel Gabriel's message to Mary,

> *The Holy Spirit will come upon you and the power of the Most High will overshadow you. So the Holy One to be born of you will be called the Son of God ...*

she stopped. Addressing the ward full of Muslim women to whom such a statement was blasphemy, she said simply, "Who said that ladies?" To which there was a prompt reply, "The angel". "Well," said Rifqa, "Whether we understand this or not, we must believe it mustn't we, because angels don't tell lies."

That simple statement forestalled an anticipated argument about Christ being the Son of God. I learned – and have since passed the lesson on to scores of students whom I have lectured on Islam – that the most effective way to deal with Muslim objections to the Christian message is to anticipate them and answer them before the objection can be voiced. Doing this saves a lot of fruitless argument. Of course, one can't always do that, and I found that Musa had some good ideas about countering Muslim objections, though I had some doubts about the soundness of some of his arguments as I had sometimes in the way he opened up a discussion as we sat on the ground outside some Muslim's house in a village.

I remember one stifling hot day when there was more than the usual quota of flies buzzing round, and Musa started off – "You see all these flies? Well, they're the result of the plagues in the days of our lord Moses". Then he turned to me, "You don't have any flies in Australia, do you?" I didn't want to spoil his opening line, but I had to be truthful, so I said, "We do have a few (!) but not like this." It is possible that Musa believed that the flies in Egypt today were the result of the plagues and that they were confined to Egypt. I was never sure.

I recall another of Musa's opening gambits in our village visiting. We were sitting on the ground at the edge of a village and just in front of us was a brick kiln burning. The process of burning bricks in the villages was simple but quite effective. Rows of sun-baked mud bricks were built up into a kind of truncated pyramid with coal dust or some similar combustible material sprinkled between the rows of bricks. The whole thing was then fired from below. It took several days for the entire kiln to burn through and during this time, the owner or some member of his family sat and kept watch day and night. The reason for this as I understood it was that the fellahin[6] explained the transformation of mud bricks into hard burned bricks by believing that the heat of the fire actually turned the whole kiln into a molten mass which then cooled to

---

[6] A labourer or agricultural worker

form the solid burnt bricks. But during the molten period the kiln was believed to be unstable and an enemy, if so minded, could come along at this stage and push the whole thing over. Hence the day and night guard. Musa's opening started something like this – "This brick kiln, reminds me of *bani*[7] Adam (the sons of Adam). We are like the mud bricks created from clay. The devil is created from fire (the Muslim belief). Now when the fire acts on the kiln it turns the bricks soft so that an enemy can push them over. So, the devil, created from fire, works on the sons of Adam and makes us weak so that we can be pushed into doing all sorts of wrong things." Then Musa got going into his message. Again, I'm not sure to what extent Musa accepted the beliefs of the fellahin, but he certainly got on their wave length.

Musa was a good preacher and even preached quite lengthy sermons in public prayer. This could create difficulties sometimes for a new preacher (such as me) in Arabic. It was the custom in our Shebin church services for a member of the congregation to lead in prayer after the reading of the scriptures. If Musa happened to pray on such an occasion, he would offer the Lord an extensive commentary on whatever had been read. This could be quite embarrassing to the preacher if later on in the service he offered a different exegesis from Musa's. So, in my case, I usually deferred the reading until after I had asked Musa to lead in prayer. At least that way I had no competition in interpretation of the text.

Speaking of public prayer, I'm sure you remember the prayer which many of our Egyptian brethren prayed in the course of an opening prayer – *Ihfazna min at tashweesh wa tashattut al afkar* (keep us from distraction and wandering thoughts). I have often used this prayer myself when I have been taking services in Arabic here in Melbourne. It is nice Arabic and an appropriate prayer to say both privately and publicly.

I remember some lovely unbaptized believers from Muslim backgrounds too. In those days, we never recognised them as believers but only as inquirers – or, perhaps unjustly, as secret believers. However, many of them were anything but 'secret' about their faith. Do you remember Sheikh Sayyid from Mit Abu Ali? I remember when he first came to us as a patient at Shebin – he was the first patient from Mit Abu Ali, a large village near

---

[7] 'bani' is an Arabic word meaning son.

Zagazig. What would it be, 30 miles from Shebin? I was giving a lesson in the men's ward at that time and I remember his fierce opposition to the message and his assertion that our scriptures were corrupted; he was quite outspoken in his thoughts about this. Interestingly though, he was honest enough to admit that he had never read the Bible and he was willing to read it. So, I gave him a copy.

People making their way into the hospital

Every time I passed his bed after that he seemed to be reading the Bible and during the morning lessons in the ward he listened attentively, occasionally making remarks which showed his genuine interest. When I interviewed him before he went home, (you remember we interviewed every patient on leaving), I was convinced he had come to a very real, if simple faith in Christ. I gave him a copy of the gospel to take home, but he insisted on having a whole Bible. We never did give whole Bibles away, but in his case the desire was so obviously genuine, I gave him the one he had been reading as a patient. It became a real treasure to him, and he invited us to come and visit him in his home.

We didn't get around to visiting him until several weeks later, largely because his village was out of our 'district'. When we eventually arrived at Mit Abu Ali, we found it was a very large village of maybe 5,000 or more people. We inquired after him. To our surprise, he seemed fairly well known once he had been identified as having been to 'Harmal' hospital. "You mean the pastor?" we were asked. "No, not a pastor, a Sheikh". "Yes, that's him", they insisted and led us to a little village shop. There was

Sheikh Sayyid with a huge smile and on a shelf behind him was the Bible he took from the hospital. Then we learned the story.

All the village dubbed him *Al Qisis* (the pastor) because when he closed his shop in the evening, he would take down his Bible and read to the group who gathered around. Then he would 'explain' it to them. Thereafter, as often as he could he would come to the hospital to learn more about the Bible. He unashamedly regarded himself as a Christian – moreover a 'Protestant' -- though he always wore the dress of a Muslim Sheikh. I remember a lovely story about him, which he told me, on one of his visits to the hospital. He had travelled that morning on a bus and was sitting behind a Coptic (Orthodox) priest. Quite simply, as though it were something normal, he told us that this priest was talking to another priest and all their conversation was about the Virgin Mary, which upset Sayyid. "It was all about 'The Virgin, The Virgin' and nothing about Christ," Sayyid told us. Then he said, "At last I leaned forward and tapped the priest on the shoulder and said 'Listen Father, you Orthodox are always talking about the Virgin Mary, but us Protestants ...'" When they looked round to see the 'Protestant', there was a smiling Muslim Sheikh looking earnestly at them.

Sheikh Sayyid was a real believer, always witnessing to his faith, especially in his village, but he was never baptized. Although he must have known that believers such as Musa, whom he met frequently at Shebin, had been baptized, he never asked about baptism and I never suggested it to him. I don't know if anyone else did. I did not, for I knew that if he took that step, almost certainly he would have been expelled from his village and his influence and testimony would cease. As it was, he was known as a Christian. How many he may have influenced for Christ I do not know. Do you think I was settling for a soft option and that we should have suggested baptism to him and trusted the Lord to undertake about the matter of his future?

I have thought long and often about the question of baptism of believers from Muslim backgrounds. The Scriptures teach fairly clearly I think that baptism was the norm in New Testament times as a means of public testimony to faith in Christ. I remember however, reading many years ago a book by Graham Scroggie, I think it was, on *The Baptism of the Spirit*. In it he expressed the opinion that the majority of references to baptism in the New

Testament referred to baptism of the Holy Spirit. I would be interested to know what you as a Baptist-cum-Anglican think about the subject.

What does seem clear to me is that the quantity of water used (if used at all) was immaterial. I think it would be difficult to establish from the New Testament that immersion was practised by the early church. You have been to Jerusalem, as I have on a number of occasions, and do you think, given the water situation in Jerusalem, that 3,000 people on the day of Pentecost could have been baptized by immersion – or even adequately sprinkled? The Centurion in Acts 10 and the gaoler in Acts 16 may have had a Roman bath in their homes in which they could be immersed 'at once', but I would think it was more likely that water was poured on them by Peter and Paul respectively.

In any case, baptism by immersion was difficult in Egypt. I don't remember that any of the churches had baptisteries and, although there was plenty of water in canals and ponds to hand, to have used them would have created a riot and exposed both baptizer and baptized to the unnecessary risk of the disease of Bilharzia. The alternative we used of baptizing people in bath tubs was rather undignified to say the least. Were you present at The Home of Peace and Safety when one extremely portly female was baptized in this way? When she was immersed and the water slopped over the sides of the tub, I guess that whatever my lips were saying and my heart feeling, my mind was saying 'Eureka'. It was quite a job levering her out of the tub afterwards. I am sure it would have been just as scriptural and much more dignified, to have poured water over her head while she knelt.

In all my reading of scripture it is evident that the significant part of the rite of baptism was not the water per se, but the public testimony expressed by the act of baptism. This of course is the significance of the ceremony of confirmation where baptism and public testimony and covenant are separated by a relatively long period, the former testifying to the faith and dedication of the parents and the latter concerned with the faith and dedication of the individual himself.

What introduced this long digression is to say that to me, the fact that Sheikh Sayyid was not baptized was not so important as the fact that he publicly and openly identified himself with Christ and the church and boldly witnessed to his faith in Christ. I would like to have your views on this subject which I have never set down in writing before.

Before leaving this subject of unbaptized believers, you would remember of course the other Sheikh Sayyid from Tunisia. He was of the Sunussi royal family and a close relative of King Idreis, who came to Egypt as a refugee when Italy annexed Tunisia between the two world wars. Sheikh Sayyid As Sunussi was, you will recall, quite a regal figure when we first met him. It was pathetic in a way that he had to live on charity because it would have been unthinkable that a member of a royal household should work. He too came to faith in Christ while a patient at Shebin hospital.

Although he was a very definite witnessing believer, he was never in quite the same league as Sheikh Sayyid from Mit Abu Ali. He comes to mind because his experience is an illustration of the part dreams still play in the life of people in the Middle East. As I read and talked with Sheikh Sayyid about the truths of the scripture, he was always stumbled by the doctrine of the Trinity. Then I remember one day how he came along to the hospital beaming. "It's all right now," he said. "I understand about the Trinity." Whether he did or not, he seemed quite convinced.

When I asked him how he came to be so sure, he told me he had gone to bed thinking about the subject and had had a dream. In his dream he saw three ropes come down from heaven. While he looked, the three ropes plaited themselves into one rope and then this one rope was pulled up into heaven again. That dream settled his doubts and he had no problem about the Trinity after that.

You remember that when Tunisia was liberated in the closing years of the war in North Africa, Sheikh Sayyid went off back to Tunisia with a letter of introduction from us to the British occupying forces. (If I remember rightly we sent it to Norman Anderson who was at that time involved about the future of Tunisia). I never heard anything more about him. Did you?

There were other believers of much humbler origins whom I remember well. Do you remember Mahmud Sultan, a very simple fellow from the villages who served for a while at the Farm Colony and for a much longer time as a cleaner at the hospital? His faith was very real and if we helped him, he helped us too with his wide range of proverbs, which I found very helpful in clarifying issues in discussions with Muslims and sometimes in getting me out of sticky situations.

Two come to mind just now: *Ibn il wizz 'awwam* (The son of a duck is a swimmer), something I suppose akin to "Like father, like son", and one that often produced a guffaw from worldly-wise fellahin and which was useful in demonstrating the futility of depending on works for salvation, *nisalli il fard wi nin'ub il ard* (we say the ritual prayers, then we go and steal from the land). Judging by the response I always got from that one, it must have cut close to the bone with regard to well-known sheikhs who regularly prayed five times a day but were not renowned for their honesty. That, coupled with the story of the Pharisee and the Publican always seemed to strike a chord with the fellahin.

Incidentally, I'm sure you found, as I did, how very true to life were the Lord's parables and how easy it was to use them as a way for a message to fellahin. How well, for instance, they could relate to the story of the Prodigal Son – how disgraceful it was to demand his inheritance while his father was still alive and the utmost disgrace of feeding pigs. You remember when we mentioned 'pigs' we always had to add hurriedly *Min gher m'akha* (no offence meant). And for the father to welcome home such a son in such a way was unbelievable. I guess they felt more kinship with the elder brother. The love of God for sinners was something amazing to our Muslim friends.

The War Years – 1939-1945

The war years inevitably made an impact on the work and witness of missions in Egypt. There was very little 'war damage' to the country and we did not experience any great hardship over rationing. But we were constantly made aware of the conflict by the presence of thousands of allied troops stationed in Egypt. Egypt was the base for all of the North Africa campaigns and for many of the Middle East campaigns, too.

The presence of all these English-speaking men – and women – from our own home countries added another dimension to our work. Those of us who were located within a reasonable distance of Cairo or the Canal Zone – and that was most of us – were involved in entertaining the troops based in these areas on top of our normal work among the Egyptian people. Most of those we entertained were New Zealanders or British, with the occasional Australian or South African.

Some of our missionaries were siphoned off into the Armed Forces or welfare work among the troops, but not many. Dr. Farrow and Norman Anderson joined up about the middle of 1940 when the situation was perhaps at its most critical in Egypt; at about the same time Brenda Nott and Celia Tucker became involved in Welfare work. A little later, probably early in 1942, Hammie and Susan started the Homely Club for the troops in Cairo. But that was the lot I think. In fact, if I remember rightly, the British military authorities gave us the distinct impression that we were of more value to the Allied cause as missionaries than as soldiers. This was my own case.

Not long after we were married, when it was on the cards that all British civilians were to be evacuated to South Africa, we decided that I would be more usefully employed in the forces than in sitting on South African beaches. So, I applied to the Royal Engineers, thinking that there perhaps my experience as a structural draftsman might be acceptable. However, I told the officer in charge that I was a missionary called to Egypt and so long as missionary work was possible I felt my place was there, but if it were no longer possible, I would want to serve where I could be most useful. The officer wasn't very enthusiastic (neither was I) but he took all my particulars. It was not until some weeks later that I got a communication offering me a position as a sergeant draftsman. By then the situation had improved and in view of the Army's lack of enthusiasm about the matter, I did nothing more about it. Some years later Norman Anderson told me that if I had volunteered for the Intelligence Service, my knowledge of Arabic and the people would have got me a commission right away. Anyhow I wasn't really interested in a commission or anything else in the Army. But I did learn one thing I hope, from the experience and that is, volunteers who attach conditions to their offer aren't really acceptable in any sphere of service.

Of course, there was Sister Agnes Schirok – a German and a Friendenschort sister – who was put under 'house arrest' at the hospital at Shebin for the duration and not allowed to travel anywhere except with special permission from the police. I don't remember to what extent, if any, we were responsible for her. She was never any embarrassment to us anyhow and the allied troops who used to visit us accepted her without any question. (You remember that Ibrahim our male night nurse, used to refer to her as 'Sister Agonies'). Her English was quite good with a trace of German accent, but I remember on one occasion in our weekly prayer meeting, she was very concerned that some of our Egyptian nurses were not going on with the Lord as much as they might and she earnestly prayed that they might "burn their britches behind them".

This brings up (in the peculiar way my mind works) the subject of speaking by translation and the perils this has when the translated speaker uses proverbs, colloquialisms and other forms of speech which don't go over in the other language. I think that speaking by translation is something no career missionary should ever do if he is working in a situation which demands the use of the language of the people. If he is not prepared to learn the language, he should go home. However, sometimes there are visiting speakers who have a real message and this must, of necessity, be translated. In such cases, it is imperative, I believe, that they should prepare a full manuscript, stick to it and go over it in advance with the translator (interpreter) so that pitfalls can be avoided.

I remember hearing of the experience of one of the members of the 'original seven' who founded EGM. Was it Mr Swan? In the early days, of necessity they had to speak by interpretation and this particular missionary had a powerful sermon on the will of God – specifically, *The I Wills of God*. He based his sermon on Genesis 12:2ff - *I will* bless you ... *I will* make your name great ... . Unfortunately, these verses are in the simple future tense in Arabic with no mention whatever of the will of God and no way of emphasising *I will*, because it just isn't in the text at all. What does a translator do in this case? He may try to make an explanation as he translates (which could take a long time and which could rob the message of its point anyhow) or he could cut the gordian knot as some quick-witted translators do, and insert his own version of the subject. Some in such cases have preached a parallel, but different message from the speaker. This has obvious perils, but what does one do?

I remember a similar sort of situation which happened when we were translating the IVF Bible Commentary into Arabic. We assigned various books or articles to different Arabic-speaking people whose command of both Arabic and English was very good, to translate into Arabic. There was a revision committee of half a dozen of us equally divided between English-speaking and Arabic-speaking people who were reasonably fluent in both languages, to go carefully through the translation to ensure that it faithfully represented the English original. I remember one translator who had strong doctrinal views of his own (of which we were not aware when we asked him to translate a particular book) which conflicted with the interpretation of the writer whom he was translating. So, he just altered the text to 'correct the errors' of the writer. Obviously that translation does not appear in the Arabic commentary.

But while I'm on the subject of the IVF commentary, I remember we had a very competent translator doing Proverbs, but he stumbled over a comment which the English commentator made on Proverbs 6:12-19. The commentator wrote – *This is a vivid portrait of ... The Perfect Bounder.* The translator came up with the Arabic equivalent of *This is a vivid portrait of a champion high jumper.* All of which shows how careful one has to be in preparing messages for translation (though of course the IVF commentary wasn't written with that in mind) and underlines my contention that messages intended for translation should be written out in full and checked over with the translator before delivery.

Colloquialisms – especially American colloquialisms – rarely are translatable, and proverbs well-accepted by an English-speaking community, may be meaningless and even quite offensive in Arabic. Nor, of course, is the English perspective of current events necessarily the same as the Arabic-speaking listeners. I made that mistake myself once in commenting on the Kikiyu situation in Kenya during the struggle for independence.

To come back to the war, however. The presence of so many allied troops in Egypt opened up two new avenues of service: witness to the troops themselves and to the hundreds of Egyptians who were employed at the various army bases. A number of the Egyptians working on the bases also lived there and had much free time with little to do in it. As the bases were technically 'British' territory, there was a greater freedom to witness to Muslims there, as well as a greater willingness of the Muslims and others to listen. Regular services for the Egyptian workers were held on some bases.

In the forces, themselves, there were a considerable number of Christians and in many cases, they formed Christian fellowships. The New Zealanders, stationed at Maadi, you remember, had a very strong fellowship which included a first-class male voice choir and a Christian Endeavour Society. These two groups visited the hospital at Shebin on a number of occasions. Now and then we had bi-lingual C.E. meetings at which our Egyptian Endeavourers and the troops participated. It was very good for our young people to realize that they were not an isolated group but part of a world-wide fellowship. It was good for the troops too to realize that here were young people endeavouring to live for Christ and the Church.

The Forces choir also gave concerts on one or two occasions at the hospital. On one particular occasion, the leader announced (in English) the numbers they were singing and as many of the hymns have also been translated into Arabic, we translated into Arabic, the announcement made by the leader so that our Egyptian staff could follow what was being sung. After one such programme at which the leader had announced that they were singing "Jesus

Lover of my Soul" to the tune of Aberystwyth, Sitt Hayat came up to me and said how much she had enjoyed that particular item. She said it was a lovely tune but why did they call it *khabar iswid* (bad news) which was what the choir leader's pronunciation of 'Aberystwyth' sounded like to her.

Of course, at the welfare centres established by the Mission to Mediterranean Garrisons (MMG) and the Homely Club run by the Hamills where our missionaries were serving, there was considerable spiritual activity in addition to the services provided for the troops. Many Christians serving in the armed forces found a deeper and more real fellowship in these centres than they had ever known at home as well as many vital opportunities to reach out to non-Christians. The MMG, in particular, had annual conventions attended by quite large numbers of service personnel. You will remember that we were often invited to give Bible studies at these gatherings. What was the MMG's Director's name – Mrs Botham? She was quite a character anyway.

If the presence of the troops in Egypt opened up a new door of service for us missionaries, it also gave the troops a new perspective on missionary work. We hoped that some of them might return after the war as missionaries. A few did, but they were almost balanced by the loss of some of our young ladies who married into the forces and returned home.

Most stations and missionaries had 'regulars' who visited us quite often and made themselves part of a family. We had some very lovely ladies at Shebin who gave the troops a feeling of home. They never forgot the graciousness of Dr. Melita Marley and the winsomeness of Dr. Mary Wills. Over twenty years later when we were on deputation work in New Zealand, we had a re-union of the Maadi Forces Fellowship when twenty or more of the old fellowship and their wives gathered to recall times and people in Egypt during the war years. Their appreciation of Dr. Marley, in particular was still very warm.

We had a group of 'regulars' who used to visit us at our home but then, as now, my ability to fit names to faces was pretty poor. So when a group suddenly arrived at our front door, I would say "Come in fellows. Hang your hats up in the hall." Then while Elsie was making them at home, I would creep out and inspect the names in their hats.

Looking back, I can't remember much about the war years, but I guess they were a watershed in the history of 'British' missions. During the years in which we entertained allied soldiers in our homes we must have become increasingly identified in the eyes of the nationalistic Egyptians at least, with the hated imperialistic powers. Whereas prior to the war *kalam Ingileez* (the word of the English) was a synonym for honesty and truthfulness, after the war the 'English' were more and more seen as procrastinating over the promise to evacuate the country, and after the Israeli war of independence in 1948 the slogan began to appear everywhere – *Al Gila' bi dim* (evacuation with blood). We would not have done otherwise than seek to provide a 'home atmosphere' for our own troops, even if we had been able to forsee the possible consequences, but those consequences were there, and eleven years after the end of the war we were out of the country for good – at least those of us who were present at that time.

Institutions

While direct evangelism was not impossible in our day, outside of Christian institutions and churches it was difficult, except on a small scale in visits to homes in towns and villages. It was possible in Christian villages, of which there were not many in the Delta where most of our work was located, to have larger gatherings for special occasions, and scripture distribution, though often subject to opposition from fanatical groups, was possible, as the Christian scriptures are regarded by Islam as being inspired exactly as is the Qur'an. Christian radio was then in its infancy and in any case did not cover Egypt. So it was that most of our evangelistic work was done as an adjunct to institutional work – medical or educational.

It was in our schools, hospital and village clinics that the door was opened to witness both within the institutions and in follow-up. However, it would be wrong to regard institutional service simply as a means to an end. I suppose there were some among our home supporters who regarded it largely in that way, but those involved in these ministries really saw in the ministry itself an avenue of Christian service and an opportunity to demonstrate the love of Christ in action. As I think of our people working in hospitals, clinics and schools, I remember them as a dedicated group of people anxious to share their skills and their faith with others.

I personally had very little experience in educational work and most of my time in Egypt was in connection with the hospital at Shebin el Qanater. It was as the *Mudir Idary* (administrator) of the hospital that I was introduced to people as we visited in the surrounding villages. That of course was my official job, though I was also responsible for the evangelistic work. If I remember rightly, there were about 60-80 villages ranging in population from a few hundred inhabitants up to several thousands, within a ten-mile radius of the hospital. In all that area and far beyond, the fame and skill of the medical people at *Harmal,* as the hospital was known, opened doors of acceptance to the message of the gospel. We had a capacity for 100 beds for in-patients, mainly in 20-bed wards, and on admission days the capacity was often exceeded.

Something like 150 or more out-patients attended the thrice-weekly clinics. The doctors normally operated twice a week and there were often visiting days twice a week. It was on the 'off' days – days when there were no outpatients – that we regularly visited in the villages following up our patients. The medical staff, missionary and Egyptian, tried to be free to participate in this renewed contact with ex-patients and their families and friends. You too, of course had some years of experience in this work at Shebin.

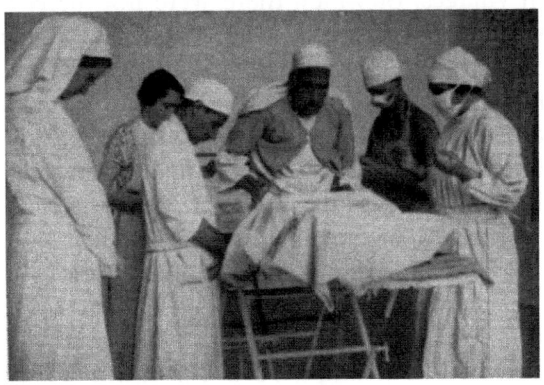

Praying prior to an operation

In many ways I think our evangelistic work at Shebin was unique. There were many things that we shared with other mission hospitals in our approach and method of working – and we had those annual (or was it bi-annual?) conferences of mission medical people to share our experience and concerns and indeed some things we 'borrowed' from them, as for instance the use of large bible posters in all the wards, which we changed every day to correspond with the programme of lessons in the wards. This idea we borrowed from the American Mission Hospital at Tanta. But there were some quite distinctive features of our methods which were peculiar to Shebin. There was our 'hospital song' which was exclusive to Shebin and became quite a trade mark – *Ya Rabbi naddif 'al by ...* (O Lord, cleanse my heart ...) and I reckon there was not another hospital where the singing was accompanied by a trumpet. The patients liked it.

Do you remember out-patients' lessons? The crowd of men waiting in the open-air shelter outside the O.P.D.? (The women of course were in a separate waiting room). It was a great opportunity to preach the gospel to Muslims often against the background of tempered opposition since, in fact, they were our 'guests'. They were a mixed crowd, mainly Muslims, comprising fellahin for the most part, but always with a sprinkling of Sheikhs who could be counted on to voice their objection to the message.

I remember one occasion when I felt absolutely exhausted and defeated by a particularly vocal and aggressive Sheikh, and I came away from the meeting feeling that nothing of the message had got across. As I walked away, this Sheikh came after me. I thought – "Here goes, another session of abuse and argument." When he caught up with me he asked if he could have a word with me. Then he said, "Don't worry about what I said in the meeting. I had to do that because of this (and he touched his *amma* – Muslim Sheikhs head-dress), but in fact, I agree with what you say and I'd like to know more." It was a lesson to me not to judge the quality or strength of the opposition by decibels.

I think it was in our follow-up work though that we were different from most medical institutions. All patients on discharge were individually interviewed – the men by you or me (whoever happened to be stationed there at the time) and the women usually by the Matron. In our final chat with them we 'graded' them according to the degree of their interest in the messages and their understanding of the gospel. On the back of their filing cards, notes were made to help in follow-up. Those who seemed to have believed in a real sense, we called 'Star patients', you remember. We systematically visited our ex-patients in all the surrounding villages and generally received an enthusiastic welcome and a readiness, if not eagerness to hear more of the message.

There were exceptions, of course, and I remember being hounded out of more than one Muslim village. Fortunately, there are few stones in the Nile Delta, so on the odd occasion they 'stoned' us it was usually with lumps of dried clay. But they could be pretty solid, though.

After writing the last page, I received a letter from Dr. Melita Marley, now in retirement (I think she is just on 90 now) in Canada. Apropos of nothing, she recalled one of our visits in the villages. She wrote (I quote),

"I remember you Aubrey so vividly at one of our visits to a nearby village. You men entered the village another way from us women. Soon we found our listeners restless and they started to urge us to leave the village as rumours arrived about the villagers attacking our fellow missionaries. When we arrived on the road we witnessed a stone throwing. You, Aubrey were catching the stones so rapidly and with a friendly face that seemed to amuse the opposition. Still, Musa Effendi got his face cut, and we arrived on our compound praising God for His protection."

I don't remember having a very 'friendly face', and I am sure was not 'amused' but I do remember fielding most of the 'stones' thrown at us. Musa, unfortunately, had never played cricket so was not as good at catching them.

But back to what I was saying. You, no doubt, remember the thrill of our 'Star Patients' conferences. Two or three times a year about 100 of our most interested ex-patients were invited back to the hospital for a day's conference. There was singing, testimonies, messages and a hot dinner. And, of course, there was always the excitement when people recognised one another. They were great occasions. How often too, we were glad to have Sheikh Kamal Mansur with us to meet and speak with the men. He understood them so well and talked with such simplicity and conviction born out of his own experience. How good it was for the star patients – often alone in their village – to meet with others of like faith. How Sheikh Sayyid enjoyed these conferences and used them to tell of his own experience. I wonder how many, unknown to us, went on to a real faith in Christ.

I don't suppose our schools operated much differently from Evangelical schools anywhere and it wasn't until after the war that we attempted something new – The Farm Colony Bible School. Some of us, you remember, had become very concerned about the problem of how to help the fellahin believers from Muslim backgrounds to maintain themselves. The problem was that when any Muslim took a definite stand for Christ, and especially if he was baptized, the very least that could happen would be rejection of him by the village and most likely, expulsion from it. How could such a person find a living and support his family, supposing that they were willing to join him? Apart from the fact that it was undesirable to employ such people with the mission, there were very few jobs that they could do – cleaners, door-keepers and so forth – and there was a definite limit to the number of people who could be employed like that – and it didn't hold out much of a long-term prospect in any case.

You remember how we discussed many times at the Field Council the suggestion I had made of what we called a Farm Colony Bible School. The idea was to establish a small farm where these believers – and their families – could live and work at a job they knew and be taught more efficient ways of working and supplementary means of livelihood such as bee-keeping, etc. At the same time, they could be given regular Bible teaching geared to their ability to receive it. You remember that finally I was asked to write an article for the EGM News outlining the project, which I did, stressing the fact that for success we needed a fully qualified agriculturalist to head it up.

And you will remember how Lord Macleay saw that article and was impressed with its potential and sent us a large donation to get it started. And that was where we made our big mistake. We took this as guidance to get moving – and we were wrong. We were wrong practically, but it was only some years after we retired that I realised how wrong we were spiritually too. I had been asked to lead some Bible studies at the church we attend in Melbourne, and it was as I was studying Paul's letters to the Church at Corinth that I was struck by what is recorded in 2 Cor 2:12-13. Let me put it down –

> *"Now when I went to Troas to preach the gospel of Christ and found that <u>the Lord had opened a door for me</u>, I still had no peace of mind because I did not find my brother Titus there. <u>So I said goodbye to them</u> and went on to Macedonia."*

I realised how easily we assume that because the Lord has opened a door for us that indicates His will. That was the mistake we made. Paul needed an open door <u>plus Titus</u> and without Titus he had no peace and left to go elsewhere. Lord Macleay's gift seemed to us the open door – but we had no Titus – no agriculturalist – and we should have waited. But we didn't. Instead, the Field Council (of which I was a member) decided, in its 'wisdom' to appoint me (who had raised the matter in the first place, but who had no agricultural knowledge at all) to get the project going, and sent me off on a crash course to the American Mission Agricultural Department at Assiut.

The Farm Colony was a disaster as far as its original intention was concerned, but we did learn some valuable lessons in other ways. I remember one thing I learned was how to build with unbaked mud bricks. We had decided that all the residences at the colony would be of mud brick to which the fellahin were accustomed and outwardly would be of the same size with more hygienic internal arrangements. As we were to live among them, our house had to conform to this pattern too. But in our case, the internal arrangement of the walls was quite distinctive as we had literally to build the walls around our furniture. We managed it, but not before I had learned an important principle about building with unbaked bricks. I remember carefully building the outside south wall beautifully vertical with a plumb line. Next day when I came back, the wall was leaning out about a foot from the vertical. What had happened was that the mud mortar on the outside of the wall which was in the full, hot sun all day had dried much quicker than on the inner side in the shade. That meant that each course of bricks had a very slight outward slope as the mortar dried and contracted on the outside but not on the inside. We had to pull the whole wall down and start again, leaving empty spaces in the mortar for the hot air from outside to get inside and make the drying process uniform. So I learned that a plumb line, even when correctly used, doesn't necessarily guarantee a vertical wall unless other conditions are fulfilled. Perhaps that has a spiritual lesson too.

One thing I did become quite skilled at was bee-keeping. With some help from an experimental farm nearby and some books on the subject, we were able to produce more honey than we could dispose of. But once again, we had to learn that it's not easy – and perhaps not desirable – to convince the fellahin that modern methods are preferable to what he knows. We had some interesting experiences though.

I remember, at the beginning of the project I had half a dozen hives at the hospital in a corner down by the generator. On one inspection, I noticed one of the hives had a large number of drones – an indication that there was no queen. There were two problems: to get a new queen and to reduce the number of the drones.

The book told me that to reduce the number of drones, I had to move the hive sideways a couple of inches each day for about ten days. The worker bees, whose homing instincts would always bring them back to within an inch or two of the spot they left to go out foraging, would adjust to the new position each day. If I had moved it the full twenty inches or so in one go, they would not find the hive. This was what would happen to the drones who did not go out to work. If they were suddenly tipped out they would go back to where the hive was when last they were outside, which would be a couple of feet from its new position. They would then fly round and round the old spot till they were exhausted and died. That was the idea. So I proceeded according to plan.

After ten days it was time to tip all the bees out of the hive as far as possible from their present site and replace the hive on the new site. So, having doped them with smoke, I removed them as far away as I could, which was outside the doctor's house about 100 yards away wouldn't it be? Then I tipped them all out and replaced the hive on the new stand. My expectation was that the worker bees would instantly return home. But there were two snags: the bees didn't understand my plan, and I didn't understand that the bees have a 'work ethic'. Since they were not due home until about sunset, for some hours, thousands and thousands of them circled round and round the doctor's house. At four o'clock Doc. Harrow came to his back door to do the afternoon round of the wards and was met by thousands of very annoyed bees. He hastily shut the door and tried the front door. Same result. At length I saw what was happening and put a veil over to him to enable him to get out.

I don't think I was too popular with the Doc for a while. But I did understand a little more clearly – and I'm sure Doc did too – what the psalmist felt like when he said of his enemies – "They surrounded me on every side ... they swarmed around me like bees" (Psalm 118:12).

While on this subject of new methods, it was during the war years – or shortly after – my memory's a bit hazy on that – that we were introduced to some small but useful new tools in presenting the message. Do you remember the name of the American missionary who introduced flannel graphs to the world? As I remember she was working in Jerusalem and made the 'remarkable discovery' that 'flannelette on flannelette sticks', and that was what she called her new visual aid. It was not until after the idea was widely taken up that the word 'flannel graph' was coined. There were modifications introduced. While the base usually remained flannelette, we found that other substances would also stick. I used blotting paper which stuck quite well and was much more rigid. We used these flannel graphs extensively, especially with children's meetings and in the villages.

Then do you remember the introduction of Gospel Recordings? Another lady missionary was responsible for this. Adly Fam made most of the Arabic records we used. We used these a lot too, mostly as 'starters' in groups we had had little or no contact with before. Out in the villages they often referred to them as 'radio' as very few had gramophones or had even heard one. Adly's voice and style was so much on their level that they quickly attracted a crowd. Then it was easy to follow up. The original recordings were on 10" records at 78 rpm so the messages were too short to stand on their own, but were an excellent introduction. I can still hear Adly's voice now. He was a great speaker.

Perhaps this is the place to recall our Boys Camps at Borrolos. Do you remember the first camp? And the prospectus Adly wrote out for us in well scripted Arabic – especially the key phrase designed to keep parents' minds at rest – "The boys will sleep ... as will the officers ... on comfortable mattresses." These 'comfortable mattresses' were palliases filled with straw which soon became most uncomfortable when the sand on which we slept penetrated the hessian and formed lumps in all the wrong places. We quickly found that the most comfortable way to sleep on the sand, was to dispense with the palliases, lie directly on the sand and wriggle about until the sand accommodated to the contours of one's body. Most campers followed our example, though some still preferred the 'comfortable mattresses'.

What an experience that first camp was! You, Noel and I were teamed with Adly, Baleegh, Abdel Mesih (Messihy) and Gubran as officers with – how many boys did we have – 30? Our camp was right on the shores of the tideless Mediterranean just a few yards from the water's edge, which made the problem of washing up simple – each camper simply took his utensils and plates to the sea and washed them up. (We weren't too pollution conscious in those days!) Do you remember the occasion when Messihy got out of his depth in the sea and could have drowned, I suppose, if you had not rescued him? I can still see him in his (literal) neck-to-knee costume stretched out on the beach exhausted and listless, and Baleegh coming up and saying in his best English as he looked on Messihy's prostrate form, "We do thank our Lord for this". It was really a bit ambiguous but we understood what he was thanking the Lord for.

Do you remember those two Muslim brothers who came to camp complete with their own personal servant? They were not very happy when we drafted him into the kitchen and made the boys do their own fatigues – nor were their parents. You remember too that we censored the campers' letters home with their knowledge and permission, before we posted them. We did this because many were Muslims and we had to be careful about the reports that went home. There was never any problem though. At that time, we were still language students and our standard of Arabic was not up to a full comprehension of handwritten Arabic, so Adly usually read them and gave us a translation. Remember the boy who wrote home and reported (in Adly's translation – "My dear reverend father, Suleiman Effendi Boulos, I am in a tent with the notable sons of *Qisis* (Pastor) Marcus ..."? They certainly were notable!

And what about that moonlit evening when we were sitting on the sand dunes, singing choruses and quoting verses of scripture? Gubran did not notice the boy behind him surreptitiously digging a hole in the sand to trap him. I can still hear Gubran saying in reverent tones *Allah muhabba* (God is love) at the moment he was undermined and fell backward into the hole, and his remark as he did so was, "I'll wallop you, boy!" – *Allah Muhabba*!

Maybe here it is appropriate to say a word about the Egyptian Delta Light Railway. This was a system of narrow gauge lines (about two feet six inches if I remember rightly) which criss-crossed the delta providing transport for people and goods away from the three or four main government railway lines. It was owned and operated by a British company. They had a timetable but it didn't function very effectively once the train left the terminal station – usually connected to a station of the Egyptian government railways. There were several reasons for that. First of all, it was a very friendly, unconventional service and didn't mind waiting a few minutes for a prospective passenger to catch up with it and secondly, there were no brakes on the train (of about half a dozen carriages) except on the engine. The guard at the rear end of the train may have had a hand brake, but I'm not sure of that. At any rate, it meant that the train could not stop suddenly and had to start slowing down a considerable distance from where it intended to stop. It also meant that the whistle blew almost continuously to warn people who might be in the vicinity that it was coming, so that they could get themselves and their animals out of the way.

But perhaps the main reason for the uncertainty of the time of arrival was the fact that there were no signals on the line. It was a single track and trains could only pass at certain stations where provision was made for that. So, to avoid collisions they had a simple system. On arriving at a station, the engine driver and his mate got off the train and went to the station master's office to get permission (*izn*) to proceed. The station master would telegraph to the next station along the line and, if there were no other trains on the line coming in the opposite direction he would give the all clear and the driver would be given a permit (*izn*) to proceed. However, away from the watchful eyes of the 'English' officials, there was no need to hurry about this, so the whole operation was usually preceded by a friendly cup of coffee and a chat, after which they would get on with the business. The result was that no one knew when the train would arrive at its destination and no one seemed to worry very much.

You remember that when you and I went on our exploratory trip to Borrolos (the most northerly tip of Egypt) to investigate the possibility of a camp there, we had to travel from Mansoura on the Egyptian railways by Delta Light to Baltim. Baltim was the northern terminus of the line and was about an hour's donkey ride from Borrollos on the coast. I'm not sure of the distance from Mansoura to Baltim, but I know it took several hours – most of the day in fact. I remember that on this occasion, we got tired of the slow trip after a few hours and went along to the engine and asked if we could ride with them on the footplate. They had no objection and indeed seemed very happy to have us with them. Having observed this practice about the *izn*, I remember your taking control at the next station, Hal. As we drew in you stood on the footplate and shouted to the station master – *Hat il izn*

(Bring the permit), just as the driver normally did. Only, this time, the station master assumed that we were British officials from the company on an inspection tour so the coffee drinking and chat were omitted and in a few minutes the *izn* was produced and we were on our way. We followed this procedure at every station thereafter. I don't think the engine driver was too pleased about it and I remember that the station master at Baltim was surprised when we arrived there considerably earlier than he had expected.

Do you remember too, when we held the camp, that you and I went on the day before with an advance party to set up the camp and Noel was to come the next day with the campers? Late in the afternoon of the second day we spotted the caravan of donkeys and camels coming over the sand dunes, but Noel was not with them. We couldn't get much information from the boys except that Mr Hunt had stayed behind at Baltim and would come early the next day. We were a bit concerned, you will remember, and thought Noel might be unwell and unable to face the donkey ride from Baltim to the camp. We envisaged him having to spend the night in the cockroach and bug-infested Greek hotel where we had spent a night on our exploratory trip, and subsequently decided that one of us should go to Baltim the next day to see what had happened. (It was already dark by this time and no donkey owner would make the trip in the dark). As we were about to set off the next morning we saw someone in the distance coming over the sand dunes on a donkey and behold, it was Noel, not looking at all unwell and grinning happily.

He told us that it happened that the British Area Director for the Delta Light was on a tour of inspection on that train and was travelling in his own special sleeping car. Noel had spent most of the journey with him and when they reached Baltim, the official suggested that Noel spend the night with him and go to Borrollos early next morning, which was what happened. Noel informed us it was a *fursa azima* (a great opportunity). Knowing Noel, no doubt he did have an excellent opportunity to share his faith with the benighted Englishman and incidentally, spend one night less on the 'comfortable mattress' at Borrollos.

But to go back to the subject of new methods of work. I suppose the one with the greatest potential for demonstrating and preaching the love of Christ was the literacy campaigns which were just gaining momentum about the time we were expelled from Egypt. They were the child of Dr. Frank Laubach. The excellent work he did throughout the world has somehow been eclipsed by Wycliffe. Althea, you remember, produced the sketches to identify the Arabic letters. We never got around to village-wide campaigns ourselves as a mission, but some of our people were involved. If I remember rightly, our work at Herz in Upper Egypt evolved from a literacy campaign there, didn't it? One important factor in the Laubach campaigns was the backing of the government anxious to increase literacy among the illiterate fellahin. The principal emphasis in this work was the principle of 'each one teach one'. As soon as an illiterate fellah could read the alphabet and spell out a few words – and that usually happened within a week or two – he was enlisted as a teacher of someone else, passing on to his 'pupil' what he himself had learned, and in the same way. In this way, the number of people being taught increased dramatically by geometric progression so that in a matter of weeks, hundreds were enthusiastically learning to read and teaching others to read. Then there were the first 'readers' to which they progressed. For Christians there were gospel stories. For Muslims there were stories about a progressive fellah and his wife. We never offered the Muslims the gospel stories to read to avoid the charge of taking advantage of their eagerness to read to proselytize them. On many occasions, however, we found that the Muslims were asking why they could not have the same book as the Christians.

The American Mission had some spectacular success in their literacy campaigns in large Christian villages in Upper Egypt and were able to follow up with Bible teaching campaigns in which Kenneth Bailey was involved. (I think this, in the end, was the reason for the Egyptian government expelling him).

We were never able to operate on that scale in our mission, partly because of a shortage of personnel, but mainly because our field of operation was in the Delta – about 98% Muslim – where a Christian village was a rarity. But we did do a lot of small-scale, mostly individual teaching. That was thrilling too, to see adult illiterates overjoyed at being able to accomplish the impossible – to read in their own language. However, such small-scale efforts lacked the momentum of a village-wide campaign. If I remember rightly, we were in the process of planning to do something on a village-wide scale when we were expelled from Egypt. I can't remember precisely what we had planned. My memory is a bit hazy on that. Perhaps your memory is better than mine.

I suppose this is an appropriate spot to recall how great a part prayer played in the life of the mission in Egypt. EGM of course was born in a half-night of prayer in Belfast in 1897. I believe the original document of committal signed by those twelve young business men is still in our London HQ. How did it run? "Lord, I am at Thy disposal for missionary service whenever and where ever Thou dost call me," followed by the twelve signatures. It was something to that effect. It was a continuing challenge to successive generations of missionaries who served in Egypt.

We followed closely the example of CIM in these matters too and our 'Faith Principle' was modelled much on CIM as, I suppose was the case with many other 'Faith Missions' as we were known in those days. Incidentally, the term 'Faith Missions' was not a term that many of us were comfortable with. It seemed to imply that other missions which had a different financial basis were not 'Faith' missions.

When we went out to Egypt we still observed the noon hour of prayer, and of course the second Saturday in every month was always Prayer Day. Over the years both these commitments were somewhat unevenly observed, though the principle never varied.

When I arrived in Egypt in 1935, I was initially stationed at Suez with Frank and Ruth Roe. Frank's principal work at that time was a club for young men, mainly students, which opened from sometime about 4-5 pm and closed about 10 pm. That meant that Frank was free to pray at noon. The other two people at Suez were Irene Naish and Cicely Radley who operated a boarding school for girls. Because of their involvement in the teaching programme and general supervision, it was not usually possible for both of them to be free at the same time during school hours, but there was always one of them present at our noon time of prayer for the work of God in Egypt particularly.

At that time noon prayer was fairly uniformly observed on all our mission stations. (I have written 'stations' because that was what we called them then and of course we were 'stationed' at such and such a place. It was toward the end of our time in Egypt that we began to question our terminology among other things. 'Station' implied a fixed location – and maybe a 'fixed' attitude – and we were beginning to think more in terms of mobility and flexibilty, and started to refer to 'centres' rather than 'stations' – a 'centre' being a place from which one moved out, a 'station' was where one stayed put. I think after we left Egypt we always referred to our locations as 'centres'. Wasn't that so? It didn't make much difference to the work. It was mainly a matter of attitudes).

Coming back to the topic of the noon hour of prayer. The situation at the hospital at Shebin was another place where there had to be some modification in our observance. Especially on Out-patients' days, the medical staff at least were mostly flat out long past noon and rarely could any number of them get together for prayer at that time. But we felt that we should not on that account drop the practice. So we came up with a plan to fit the circumstances.

The nurses' lecture room was set apart for prayer from about noon till 1pm. On a table in the room, we put the prayer notes for the day which we used – our EGM News sheet, the Egypt Intermission prayer notes, and FFM prayer calendar. Then, as people were free they came to the room, read the notes for the day and prayed with those who were there. Did you continue that practice when you were there?

Mention of the EGM News Sheet brings up the subject of our monthly day of prayer. That was what it was originally and some people kept the whole day free for prayer right through the time we were in Egypt. But again, institutional routines bit into that time and gradually we thought of it more as Prayer Day than a day of prayer. In most centres, I guess, about 3-4 hours were spent in prayer on the second Saturday in the month, with usually a further time in the evening. For that day, we prepared a 'news sheet' and every station sent in their monthly news to HQ by a certain deadline, to be typed up and sent out to every missionary before Prayer Day. Although a copy was always sent to London HQ, I don't think it was until your time as Field Secretary that we thought of preparing the news sheet for Home consumption as well. Even then it was primarily intended to provide information for Prayer Day on the field.

I suppose it was inevitable that this emphasis on prayer should rub off on to the missionary families in one way or another. I remember the occasion when I went over to your house to discuss something with you and Roger, then about five, I guess, opened the door. I asked him if you were about and he said, "I expect he's praying." I'm not sure whether he regarded this as commendable or not, for I remember Lilian telling us that just about this time Roger had informed her that "Prayers is ghastly." I wonder where he got that word and what he meant by it?

Norman was much more positive. Lilian told us on another occasion a story about Norman when he was quite small. He asked her what he should pray about as she guided him in his evening prayers. Lilian suggested he should ask the Lord to send them some money, because we were very short at that time. So, Norman asked the Lord to send us some money. Next night he asked Lilian again what he should pray for and she again suggested that he ask the Lord to send some money. Norman looked up in surprise and said, "What? Hasn't He sent it yet?"

But to come back to our mission practice. I remember that our annual Field Conference, which lasted a week or ten days, was more properly referred to as the 'Annual Gathering'. The whole time was spent in prayer, devotions and Bible study, apart from one day, though later the time was extended a little, which was devoted to the business of mission. The principal business of the conference was to elect the Field Council which was responsible for the conduct of the business of the mission on the Field. Major items of policy were also discussed at this time.

We met at Radstock Hall at Zeitoun HQ and what times we had together in that annual gathering! Remember the large banner that was always at the back of the speaker – "That in All things He might have the pre-eminence"? I wonder what happened to that banner when we were expelled from the country. For most of the time you and I were in Egypt we had the last of the founding 'Seven' with us – George Swan. In his later years there he did not take a very prominent part in the meetings, but I remember one of the last messages he gave, where he rebuked the tendency on the part of some to idealize 'The First Seven' and to walk in 'the tradition of the Elders'. He reminded us of the apostolic injunction regarding 'whose faith follow'. It was their faith, not their methods which was important in the continuing work of EGM.

However, if the evangelistic tradition of the founding seven was not slavishly followed, a lot of their pattern of living – and eating – was established practice in the mission households when we arrived on the Field. Do you remember that in our early years – when a male missionary's allowance was 9 pound per month and a female's 8 pound – men were served up 2 eggs for breakfast and ladies one, oranges (which we had most days of the year for lunch) had to be cut in halves and eaten with a spoon, and of course we were always expected to 'dress' for dinner. Pith helmets had to be worn outside too, and our early attempts to go out bareheaded were frowned on. "And many other such things" did we do.

As I was writing that, I was reminded of the system of 'intercessory missionaries' that was operating when we first went to Egypt. These were people in the Home lands (principally UK) who covenanted to give themselves to prayer for believers from Muslim backgrounds and inquirers particularly. Each believer and inquirer was given a number and the relevant information concerning each one of them was passed on to the intercessory missionary. As particular problems and needs were encountered this information was passed on to the intercessory missionaries under the heading of the relevant number. No names or locations were ever mentioned. This was to avoid any adverse publicity or the attention of Censors. I'm sure this specialised home ministry was greatly used. Its full effect we'll probably never know.

The scheme came to an end during the war when total censorship was imposed on all mail. Indeed, apart from the 'aerogrammes' that were introduced during the war, there was no other way to correspond with those outside Egypt. You remember those early aerogrammes? We had to go to the post office and procure printed forms, quarto size, which provided space for the name and address of the addressee and the sender. The rest of the space was used for correspondence. When complete they were returned to the post office which collected the fee and stamped them. They were then photographed along with hundreds of others on microfilm and dispatched to the destination by air. There they were enlarged back to the original size and sent to the addressee.

When normal correspondence was resumed after the war years, we never recommenced the intercessory missionary scheme. That's right isn't it? In any case our rather elementary method of passing information intelligible to the recipients but not, we assumed, to government censors, would not be very effective now, if ever it was as effective as we then believed. The Islamic Foundation in Leicester, UK, has probably more detailed information about missions and missionaries working in Muslim lands and their activities than we have ourselves.

I am of the opinion that some of our efforts to camouflage the information we send from the Field are more likely to arouse suspicion than would a straightforward statement of fact. I can't for the life of me understand why the mention of Christian names of missionaries but the withholding of some surnames is likely to do more than confuse those who pray without in the least deterring Muslim bodies from knowing what we are on about. The authorities know we are missionaries, they know we consider it our prime task to preach the gospel and if they let us into their country they don't expect us to try and disguise that fact any more than Muslims in the West disguise the fact that they seek to win people to Christ from non-Muslims. What are we afraid of?

I remember on one occasion at Shebin when the Muslim Brotherhood tried to stop us preaching to Muslims in the hospital and complained to the Chief of Police about us. The Police Chief, a Muslim, whose office you remember, was opposite the hospital, sent for me and, told me of the complaint. He was a friendly man, well-disposed towards us (I think his wife had been a patient) and obviously wanted to save us any trouble. So, after he had set out the Brotherhood's case, he suggested to me that their claim was not true – leaving me a loophole to get round the matter. However, I explained to him that we were in fact proclaiming the gospel to everyone as we consider that that message was integral to the whole process of healing the spirit as well as the body, and that it would be less than honest if we concealed from one section of the people the means of healing their greatest illness. The point is, the Police Chief conceded the point, merely suggesting that we didn't make our preaching too obvious. I don't know what he told the Brotherhood, but I believe he would not have had a great deal of respect for us if we had agreed to stop preaching the gospel. I know we need to do so without being offensive to Muslim beliefs and sincerely held attitudes, but I do believe we must not try to avoid the offence of the cross, whatever the consequences. I'd like to have your views on this subject.

Missions and Government

During the twenty odd years we were in Egypt, we experienced the whole gamut of relations to the government of Egypt from that of extra-territorial privilege to expulsion as undesirable aliens. I don't suppose any of us were happy with either extreme. The extra-territorial privileges which foreign residents enjoyed were an injustice with which we missionaries were never really happy or comfortable, but about which there was nothing we could do. Maybe it was just those of us from 'down under' who were uncomfortable with the situation. I wouldn't want to be dogmatic about that. There were undoubtedly pros and cons about this matter and probably those of us from 'down under' were more inclined to adopt a 'con' stand anyway. Maybe we were a small minority.

Whatever it was, I remember the real sense of relief it gave when extra-territorial rights of foreigners were abolished. When was it in the early war years? At last we foreigners had no privileges our Egyptian colleagues did not enjoy. Indeed, we became subject to a number of disabilities. Among the 'privileges' we no longer enjoyed was that of being subject to consular courts and not Egyptian courts. I do think however, that the British did not abuse this privilege as much as did the consular courts of some other countries. If I remember rightly citizens (and we were all that at that time) were not ipso facto immune from Egyptian law – on the contrary the British Consular courts rigorously enforced it.

Then there was the exemption from customs duties too, which was a great benefit to our institutions and indeed to us missionaries who benefited from duty-free Christmas boxes sent to us from NZ especially. When we had to pay customs, it was no longer practical to send goods either to institutions or individuals. That disadvantaged some of our less well-off supporters at Home who could not make large donations but who could and did make or provide things needed on the Field. Eventually we had to send word to our home supporters not to send 'boxes' any more as the last boxes of gifts to the hospital at Shebin cost us more in customs (even on torn sheets for bandages) than we would have to pay to purchase the goods locally. But on the whole, the plusses of the abolition of extra-territorial privileges far outweighed the minuses.

However, long before extra-territorial rights were abolished, we missionaries – just because we were Christian missionaries – were the targets of many attacks, in the Press and sometimes by legislation. At the same time, so long as Egypt was under the protection of Great Britain – and that was until the unilateral abrogation of the Anglo-Egyptian government in 1951 – pressure could be brought to bear on the Egyptian government to restrict or prohibit legislation which violated the rights of Egyptian nationals on the grounds of their religion. Occasionally legislation or government decrees prohibiting the propagation or teaching of the Christian faith to non-Christians, while not placing the same restrictions on the universal proclamation of Islam, were withdrawn. But that was only on the public official level. Otherwise there were continual attacks in the Press, from the mosques and in other ways. And there was often de facto discrimination and imposed disability without its being de jure.

The strange fact however, was that most of us went about the task of proclaiming the gospel, blissfully ignorant of much that was being said about us or plotted against us. Because we were generally well-received by those amongst whom we worked – particularly in the Delta – we were unaware of the rising tide of anti-Christian and anti-missionary propaganda and plotting especially by the fanatical Muslim Brotherhood. A lot of that was due to the fact that we did not bother (and in most cases, were not sufficiently competent in Classical Arabic) to read the Arabic papers, and a wave of opposition which had been building up for some time would suddenly burst on us and take us completely by surprise. (That was what happened, to Paul and Barnabas at Lystra. Had they known the Lycaonian language, they would have known what the crowd was saying and what they were up to. As it was, it wasn't until they were on the point of offering sacrifices to them that they knew what the crowd was doing).

To counter this and to keep all foreign missionaries *au fait* with what was happening, the Egypt inter-mission Council (of which we and most missions in Egypt were members) instituted a Press Translation Service. What happened was that certain people were appointed to read Arabic papers (perhaps once or twice a week) so that the whole of the Arabic Press (it was rather extensive) was regularly read by someone. When items of concern to missions cropped up they were translated into English and sent to the person responsible for the Service. Then every two months or so, this was circulated to all the contributing societies. If something urgent turned up, this was sent out right away.

I remember I was appointed to read *Al Balagh* once a week. *Al Balagh* (the News) was, you remember, often referred to as *Al Bala'a* – similarly written in Arabic – which could be translated as 'The Drain', or even 'The Sewer', which gives some idea of the type of news it published. I don't think it helped my spiritual life in any way, and I guess that some of our Egyptian Christian friends wondered why I bought it. But it did give me some idea of what the readers of such a paper were thinking and doing. I remember being surprised to see my name in it on one occasion. I was referred to as 'the disciple of Morrison'. Sam Morrison was then the secretary of CMS and was very much in the public eye for his missionary activities. It gave me a jolt to think that I, buried in the Delta, came under scrutiny. It must have been that I was a member of some committee or other in which Sam Morrison was active. At this distance, I don't remember exactly.

It was not only anti-mission attitudes of which we were largely ignorant, but, as I later found out, our ignorance of general political attitudes could get us into trouble. It was shortly after the war when I was seconded to the Nile Mission Press. One of my responsibilities was to produce the monthly magazine *Risalat as Salaam* (Message of Peace) produced jointly by EGM and NMP. During the disturbances leading up to independence in Kenya, I came across an article in the British Christian Press concerning an incident in Kenya. I don't remember the details now, but it concerned the Lord's protection of some Christian folk in a remote area of Kikiyu country, which I thought would be an encouragement to Middle East Christians under pressure. In the article the Kikiyu were very definitely the villians of the piece. As I remember it, I asked our friend Adly Fam if he would translate it. I remember the shocked expression on his face as he said to me, "You can't publish that. To the Egyptians the Kikiyu are heroes." How sensitive missionaries need to be to the climate of opinion round about them if they are to remain and be effective witnesses for Christ!

Although there were periodic outbursts of anti-missionary activity all the time we were in Egypt, it was not until after the war that these intensified. I guess the reason for that was not so much an increase in hatred for missionaries as hatred of the British. We were regarded as an 'English' mission and because of that we were suspected of being agents in some way of imperialism. In actual fact, the British imperial policy in general was to discourage missionary work among Muslims. They would have much preferred that we did not rock the boat too much. As missionaries per se, we never received any encouragement from the British government.

It was after the war that anti-British activity and demonstrations were stepped up, and organizations such as the fanatical Muslim Brotherhood used this as a cover for anti-missionary activities. From their point of view this was understandable, as in Islam there is no distinction between 'church' and 'state'. Islam is not simply a religion; it is an all-embracing socio-political-religious system. So, quite naturally they made the same connection between 'English' missions and the British occupying power (euphemistically called the 'protecting' power).

This all culminated in the unilateral abrogation of the Anglo-Egyptian Treaty by the Egyptian government ten years before its expiry date. From that time relationships deteriorated rapidly and we came under suspicion from nationalistic and religious fanatics, though interestingly enough, not from the authorities, who, right to the end, acted with amazing correctness and helpfulness. You will remember as vividly as I do, I'm sure, how right at the end of our time in Egypt, while we were under house arrest and just before we were expelled, those Egyptian army officers in a pick-up who rescued us from a violent mob and returned us safely to our HQ.

I think the turning point for us as a mission was October 1951 when there was the British attack on the Egyptian police post in Ismailia and several Egyptian policemen were killed. This sparked a tremendous outburst of violence against anyone and anything 'British'. Yet, even so, we were able to carry on our work as usual, and if there were plots against us we were largely unaware of it. We did become concerned, however, about the safety of some of our single lady missionaries who were relatively isolated in areas where there was a lot of tension. In particular, you remember we were concerned about Margaret Fairful (or was it Lillian Lamb?) in Tel el Kibir very near Ismailia. It was decided that you and I should run down to see how they were and if necessary evacuate them to Zeitoun for safety. You were then at HQ in Zeitoun and drove down to Shebin and picked me up. We then drove down to Belbeis – about half-way to Tel el Kibir – and called in on Hammie. For some reason, I don't remember now, we left the HQ car at Belbeis and went on to Tel el Kibir in the Belbeis car, perhaps because it was bigger if we had to evacuate the folk from Tel el Kibir. It was a perfectly innocent arrangement as far as we were concerned and we did not know that all our moves were under surveillance by the Brotherhood. The ladies at Tel el Kibir did not feel unduly in danger – they probably weren't from the local folk – and in any case were preparing to go off to Ismailia the next day for a break, so we left them there and retraced our route. We were vaguely conscious of a car tailing us most of the way, but not worried about it. We changed cars again at Belbeis and returned home.

I remember it was late the next night that you phoned me at Shebin. As you will recall, we had no direct phone in those days but were connected to the exchange at the railway station. The station master was a portly fellow and a member of the Brotherhood. We suspected that he listened in to all our phone conversations. Do you remember saying as we were speaking – "can't say much to you because there is a big fat bloke listening in." Immediately there was a click as he put his receiver down. He evidently didn't like your description of him. Then you told me the news. Apparently, our innocent change of cars the day before had aroused the suspicions of those who were tailing us, who assumed that that indicated we were up to some funny business.

That day a large crowd had stoned our mission compound at Belbeis, ransacking and looting the premises. Hammie and Susan were out paying a courtesy call on the police chief at the time and the crowd went looking for them at the mission compound. We had two single missionaries there at that time, responsible for the Girls' School, and they were in grave danger. A very brave young Christian fellow hid them behind a curtain, wrenched off a tap and held it like a revolver keeping the crowd back. After they had smashed up the premises, the crowd left, apparently en route to Shebin to smash up the hospital and deal with the 'British spies' there. If I remember rightly, after they had gone, the police chief, who apparently had been unaware of what had happened, got Hammie and Susan and the girls to Zagazig. From there they got in touch with you and you with me. I alerted the rest of the missionary staff that night and none of us got much sleep.

The next day, I went over to the police chief across the road from the hospital to discuss the situation with him. He said if a riot started and crowds surged on the hospital there was little he could do to prevent it or to protect us, but he said if we felt it right to evacuate the hospital he would give us a police escort to Zeitoun. We spent a good deal of time that day in prayer and discussion and tried to go about our business as usual – it was an outpatients day – and finally felt we should discuss the whole situation with our senior Egyptian staff. They felt that if we remained and the crowd from Belbeis did come along we could be placing the lives of our Egyptian colleagues – and even the patients – at risk, but if we were to leave they would be unlikely to be attacked. They agreed to maintain the work of the hospital for the few days we expected to be absent, so that night we left under police escort for Zeitoun – and did not return for about five or six months. The work of the hospital carried on and they were not attacked.

Eventually, you remember, as tension mounted, we had to pull in all our missionaries to Zeitoun. The last group to come was from Ismailia. Remember the lovely story about Noel? They had got safely to Port Said and spent the night there preparing to move off the next day along the relatively safe main road to Cairo. Noel went out for a walk in the evening and was immediately surrounded by a hostile mob shouting abuse and threats against the Englishman. Noel, quick-witted as he was on such occasions, protested that he was not Engeleez (English), he was a 'New Zealander'. Apparently, the crowd did not comprehend the distinction while all the while Noel continued to assert that he was 'New Zealander.' Eventually an 'educated' fellow came along and spoke to Noel who again insisted that he was 'New Zealander'. Then this chap turned to the crowd and said, "He's not Ingeleez, he's Dutch". But it was marvellous the way the Lord used all sorts of people and ways to protect us in those critical days.

After a week or so at Zeitoun while the situation began to worsen rather than ease, and it appeared likely that rather than days away from our stations, it would be weeks or months, we had to sort ourselves out. Some of us were seconded to other missions working in Cairo. In places such as CMC (Christian Mission College), the CMS hospital at Old Cairo and other places that were not at risk, security was good. Others worked at different tasks at HQ, and you and Lilian went to Sudan to explore the possibility of work there. As for the rest, about 8 or 9 were language students at various stages of study, and 2 or 3 of us had sufficient competence in Arabic to start a language school of our own, as it was not safe for them to use public transport to get into Cairo to the SOS. We all worked hard at it and held examinations at the beginning of January. The students did well and we decided that the situation was sufficiently calm for us to go to Alexandria for a few days' holiday. We set off in two cars in the early morning of January 26th, 1952, a day which beside being Australia Day, was to be one of the landmark days of Egypt.

When we arrived at the outskirts of the city of Cairo, Egyptian police diverted us and we had to make a long detour to get back on to the desert road to Alexandria. It was not till we got there several hours later that we learned that Cairo had been burned that day and everything foreign had been attacked and burned and several Britishers lost their lives. It was all starting at the time we were turned back. Had we gone by the usual route through Cairo, we would have run right into the rioting crowds. Another evidence of the Lord's protection.

We never repaired the property or re-opened the work at Belbeis, and the premises at Tel el Kibir were later attacked and looted – by British soldiers from Ismailia – while we were all up at Zeitoun. I can't remember now why they came along, but I think they thought it was a Brotherhood centre. Sometime later an interesting thing came to light. It appears that one of the British soldiers who looted our premises at Tel el Kibir took a Bible belonging to one of our missionaries. Through reading it, he eventually came to know the Lord.

When the situation calmed down somewhat and we were able to return to our stations, we began to think and plan seriously about handing over all our property to the Evangelical Church. Other missions were doing the same thing as it was becoming very apparent that the days of foreign missionary work in Egypt were running out. Our Egyptian colleagues had proved very capable of maintaining the work during our absence and we had no qualms on that score. Denominational missions such as CMS and the American United Presbyterian Mission did not have much difficulty about this, as the churches and missions were part of the same organisation. However, interdenominational missions such as EGM were in a different situation. It had been (and remains) part of our policy not to found new churches (denominations) but to co-operate with existing Evangelical Churches, but there was no administrative or organisational link with them. Our missionaries were guest members of the churches.

Consequently, when we wished, as foreigners, to hand our property over to an unconnected Egyptian organisation, there were a lot of complicated procedures. Not least of these was a considerable tax on 'gifts'. Neither the church nor we as a mission was in a position to pay the transfer fee and in the event, we were still negotiating when we were expelled from the country.

Good-bye, Egypt

After the burning of Cairo on January 26th, 1952, events in Egypt moved fairly rapidly. The Egyptian army moved in to restore order in the city and the country in general and by March, I think, we were able to return to our stations. One thing I remember on the morning of the day we were leaving Zeitoun for Shebin, was our reading together of *Daily Light*.[8] A verse in that reading stood out as a promise – "The Lord shall preserve thy going out and thy coming in from this day forth and even for ever more" (Psa.121:8).

In view of the dangers of travel in Egypt over the past months, this came as an assurance of divine protection. To this day I am convinced that the Lord has continued to protect us in travel, though I guess my guardian angel has been very busy at times. I have never felt any assurance about protection from other dangers, but I have always felt confident in travel. That doesn't absolve me from careful driving of course. For some years in Lebanon I had on my dashboard a prayer which the Lutheran Hour had produced – "Lord, grant me Thy protection and keep me mindful of my responsibilities as I drive this car."

When we got back to Shebin, it was to a new situation. For some months, the Egyptian staff had managed the affairs of the hospital exceptionally well, even though it had lacked some of the appeal the presence of the English medical staff had provided previously. They were happy to hand the administration back to us, but we felt that a new arrangement was called for. A management committee was formed in which our Egyptian colleagues had an equal say with us on all matters – medical, administrative and spiritual, with the intention of gradually increasing their responsibility. This was in operation up to the time of our expulsion from Egypt four years later. However, during those four

---

[8] *Daily Light* is a daily devotional book which is based solely on Scripture verses. For each day a number of verses relating to the theme of the introductory verse are brought together to form the reading. In some editions, there are readings for both the morning and the evening.

years, there was a feeling of increasing tension as we were willy nilly caught up in the political turmoil.

King Farouk, by this time a dissipated and increasingly unpopular monarch, removed the administration of the country, as was the custom, during the hot summer months of July and August, from Cairo to Alexandria. All the heads of government departments consequently moved to Alexandria, rendering Cairo a dead city administratively during these months, It was almost impossible to do any official business and if the fasting month of Ramadan happened to occur then (it is a lunar month shifting back eleven days every year), everything ground to a halt. So while Farouk and the government were holidaying in Alexandria in July, maintaining a facade of governing the country from there, the Egyptian army moved in and seized control of the country, first in Cairo, then in Alexandria. The coup (revolution) was organized by a group of young officers headed by Gamal Abdel Nasir (Nasser), but in order to win the approval of the populace, a benign fatherly figure, General Muhammad Nagib, was proclaimed President. He was a popular figure and continued to live in his own modest villa at Helmiah, quite near our headquarters in Zeitoun, rather than in one of the royal palaces. The whole new emphasis was on simplicity. The new military government always dressed either in uniform or coatless with white shirts (like Bob Hawke and the Labour Caucus), to indicate their purity of purpose and incorruptibility, in contrast to all the ostentation and corruption of the Farouk government. Some of the ministers were photographed riding to their offices hanging on outside of a tram like many other Cairenes. And there was the widely published photo of one of the ministers dancing with a group of Berbers in southern Egypt dressed only in his underpants, to show his brotherhood with the other dancers. He thereafter was known in the foreign press as 'The Dancing Major'. His colleagues were not too pleased about that kind of publicity and thought he went too far. Thereafter he gradually became less prominent in public life.

The new government discarded the lovely old green flag with the silver crescent and replaced it with a black, red and white one (a political equivalent of the 'wordless book'!), black for the corruption of the Farouk era, red for the sacrifice of the people (ie, the Army), and white for the purity of the new regime.

They moved to distance themselves from the Farouk era in other ways too. All honorific forms of address were abolished, not merely because of socialistic philosophy, but mainly because they were Turkish in origin. Not only did *Pasha* and *Bey* go, but also the widely used *Effendi*, which was a courtesy title for the educated – perhaps the equivalent of 'Mr'. It was officially replaced by *Sayyid* but this title was slow to gain general acceptance, mainly, I would think, because of the popular association of the word with saints of which there were quite a few venerated in Egypt. And to address someone merely by his name without a 'handle' was still considered by most people as discourteous outside the circle of very intimate friends and relatives. Only servants were normally addressed by their names without a title.

To give point to this reform, the *tarbush* or *fez*, the headdress worn by Effendis and government officials, was abolished and it was likewise forbidden to carry a fly-switch which was regarded as another adjunct of the effendi. The t*arbush* was probably not a great loss, as these unventilated flower-pot hats, though picturesque, were very hot in the summer and offered no protection from the sun. As Egyptian pastors preached with their *tarbushes* on, it was a common sight to see them during the course of a sermon when they got warmed up, having to lift them every now and then to ventilate their heads or even remove them. They required frequent re-blocking too at special establishments dotted all over the cities.

The abolition of the fly-switch was however, a distinct discomfort to almost everyone including us missionaries. Given the hordes of aggressive flies in the villages, they were an almost indispensable first line of defence. They varied in design from very simple ones of palm fibre used by the villagers to the horse hair type used by most people, including ourselves. Some were very sophisticated with polished wooden handles (the type I favoured) or even ivory or bone handles. Elsie had a very handsome bone-handled switch, I remember. Having to substitute a handkerchief for this simple 'weapon' was most unsatisfactory.

In line with the abolition of titles was the prohibition of using honorific forms of address. It was understandable that the obsequious forms of address – "Your Honour", "Your Excellency", etc addressed to officials (especially when seeking favours), should go, but with them went the courtesy title of *hadritak* (Sir, or Madam) with which all people other than servants were addressed. To address someone as 'you' was always considered discourteous and I personally never found myself able to dispense with *hadritak*, especially in addressing ladies. This 'reform' extended to the addressing of envelopes to go through the mail. Normally the addressee was addressed as *Hadrit al Fadil al Muhtaram*, which I suppose could be summarised as 'The Honourable ...'. This was not now to be done. People were to be addressed simply as *Sayyid*. But centuries of custom and the innate courtesy of the Easterner die hard and even those who conformed to the new directives continued (to the present day I think) to add *al Muhtaram* (The Honourable) <u>after</u> the name.

Muhammad Nagib was a popular figure and at Christmas time he sent out Christmas cards to all leaders, Christians and Muslims featuring Christian and Muslim symbols, stressing the unity of all Egyptians. The extremes of the Muslim Brotherhood were curbed and land reforms were instituted by making the maximum holding by any one person 50 acres and re-distributing the balance in 5 acre lots to landless fellahin. There were administrative difficulties about that, largely because the landless fellahin did not always live where re-distributed land was available, but the principle was widely accepted – except by the wealthy landowners.

This situation continued for about a year, during which Gamal Abdul Nasir was always seen in the company of Mahummad Nagib and increasingly seen as the power behind the throne. Eventually Gamal felt himself to be widely enough accepted as de facto leader to dispense with Muhammad Nagib, who was placed under house arrest and Gamal took over officially. I remember that day. I had been in Cairo for some reason or other and as I drove along the road to Shebin which went through Helmiah, quite near to Muhammad Nagib's house, I was surprised at the number of armoured vehicles proceeding out towards Helmiah. The next day we heard what happened.

I don't remember anything outstanding in the next three years as far as our work as a mission was concerned, but the political tensions between Egypt and Britain increased and the situation deteriorated. Finally, the British agreed to withdraw their troops from Egypt leaving unarmed civilian technicians and experts to supervise the safe running of the canal with a few British security men. As I remember it, none were in uniform.

The next and final chapter in the long, drawn out drama occurred when Gamal Abdul Nasir nationalised the Suez Canal. It was very well planned and executed. Egyptian soldiers were posted unobtrusively at all key installations in the canal zone waiting for the cue that was to be given them in a speech Gamal was to give to the nation. On the mention of the cue words they were all simultaneously to move in and take charge. Elsie and I were at Abu Hammad at the time and I listened in to most of his long harangue. Eventually he gave the cue (to which only the troops were privy) – "we have decided to nationalize the canal". Listening as we were, it did not mean much more than part of the rhetoric. In the canal zone, it signalled the end of foreign control by the Anglo-French company and its seizure by Egypt.

After that things became chaotic as far as Egypt and the Western world were concerned, culminating in the Anglo-French-Israeli plan to seize the canal and re-occupy the canal zone. Around about September/October 1956 things came to a head.

At that time, Wil and Zoe Poster were in charge of the Nile Mission Press and were on the verge of a breakdown, so their committee insisted on their taking a holiday in Alexandria and Elsie and I were asked to fill in at NMP for a month or so. NMP was just down the road from our EGM HQ. We ourselves had just come back from holiday, so had none of our possessions with us, but we moved in just as we were in to the Posters' flat. It was just then that the British gave notice that unless both Egypt and Israel withdrew their forces ten miles from the canal by a certain deadline, the British would bomb Egyptian airfields. It was fair enough to demand this of Israel who were on Egyptian soil, but it was naturally (and the British knew it) unacceptable to Egypt – why should they withdraw in their own country? When the deadline passed, the British announced that at a certain time their bombers would attack and civilians were advised to keep out of the area. Precisely on time they did so. Anti-British feeling ran very high from then on and as we (Elsie and I) were rather isolated at the NMP premises, we decided to move over to our HQ and I walked the half mile or so to the NMP office each day. Even that got a bit dangerous after a while, so we left the Egyptian accountant in charge and I kept in touch by phone until finally the Egyptian police seized and sealed the press.

Shortly after that, the British and French forces invaded the canal zone and a state of war existed between Egypt and Britain. All British, French and Jewish residents of Egypt were put under house arrest and all our people were brought to Zeitoun. Our phone was cut off, our bank accounts frozen, and we had to answer a police roll-call every day. Two of our Berber servants loyally stayed with us and did our shopping and cooking. By pooling all the cash we had, we managed to keep going for three or four weeks. We spent the time mainly in prayer and Bible study and in various chores about the compound.

You will vividly remember, as I do, that at that time, a British bomb attack was launched on the international airport quite near us early one morning and you went up on the roof to see what had happened. When you came down, a couple of Egyptian policemen arrested you on suspicion of being a parachutist just dropped down. When I came along and learned what had happened I went out to protest to the police and they arrested me too. You remember the howling mob that gathered around us after our blood as the police tried to get us to the police station. It seemed quite certain we'd never make it when an Egyptian army pick-up came along and rescued us from the crowd and took us off to the police station. They could have been excused if they had handled us roughly, given the fact that British bombs were falling on civilian targets at that very moment. But they treated us correctly – even courteously – and eventually returned us in the pick-up to our HQ, where prayer had been made continuously for our safety.

Only a few days after that, you, Harold Langley and your families were expelled. About ten days later the rest of us got orders to get out within 48 hours. With no possibility of getting out by road, or sea and with only one or two airlines (one of them Yugoslav) running skeleton shuttle services from the bomb-damaged Cairo airport, it wasn't easy to find an airline that could and would take our whole staff in one lift. We also did not want to be split up under the circumstances. The procuring of the required exit permits within the time limit was a problem and above all, our money was frozen. Eventually we were able to get accommodation on an S.A.S. plane and the American United

Presbyterian Mission (not affected by the crisis) kindly advanced us the money we needed. Then, after a few false starts, we eventually all got out on a plane going to Rome.

There was one last lesson I learned from that experience – how little of life's material goods are really essential. We were leaving for good – our exit visas stated that fact – and we could only take with us one suitcase, though each person was allowed up to 10 kg excess baggage. When Elsie and I came to pack up, we found extreme difficulty in filling two suitcases with what we considered absolutely essential. As a matter of fact, in the end we started adding a few things that we didn't consider essential but could be useful. When we unpacked finally in London we found we had, if I remember rightly, 4 pairs of scissors.

I remember the day, early in December, when we flew out of Egypt for the last time. It was a beautiful day and the Delta looked resplendent in various shades of green as we then headed out over the desert towards the Mediterranean. I remember the mixed feelings of relief and sadness. Relief to be away from it all at last, but sad to be leaving in this way the country to which EGM had been so definitely called 58 years before.

Good-bye Egypt.

Retrospect

I think the final word is with the Psalmist. Recently I was impressed with Psalm 77:19-20. Transferring the full stop to after 'flock' in v20, it reads "...though your footprints were not seen, you led your people like a flock." It looked very much as though it was Gamal Abdul Nasir who expelled us from Egypt, and not because we were missionaries, but because we were 'British'. It seemed to bring to an abrupt end 58 years of work and witness in Egypt, and we had to leave open so many loose ends. There was little evidence of the 'footprints' of the Lord in all of it, but much of the boot of Abdul Nasir.

Yet now, thirty-two years on, as we look back, I believe it was the Lord who led us out, though his footprints were not seen. And we really didn't leave so many loose ends, unfinished work, either. Rather, I believe we finished the work we had to do in Egypt and God had a wider work for us in the Middle East. We had laid a foundation on which our Egyptian friends and colleagues have built and built well.

Unless the Lord allowed us to be expelled as we were, we would probably have continued there, not writing new chapters but simply adding more full stops to the sentence already complete. There had to be that break in our service and we would probably never have made it ourselves, but carried on like someone past retiring age who won't retire and who hinders rather than helps the work he has been instrumental in building up.

Now, after a break of some 25 years, MECO is back again in Egypt with a new commission and, I trust, a new vision. However, I'm sure it is with the same love for the land and people our Lord expressed in the verse from Isaiah 19 which we adopted as our own desire – "Blessed be Egypt my people".

Printed by Libri Plureos GmbH in Hamburg, Germany